30-1056

WITHDRAWN

THE RIGHT OF MOBILITY

Kennikat Press

National University Publications

Multi-disciplinary Studies in the Law

General Editor

Rudolph J. Gerber
Arizona State University

THE
RIGHT
OF
MOBILITY

WITHDRAWN

GERALD L. HOUSEMAN

with a foreword by
C. HERMAN PRITCHETT

National University Publications
KENNIKAT PRESS // 1979
Port Washington, N. Y. // London

Manufactured in the United States of America

Published by
Kennikat Press Corp.
Port Washington, N. Y. / London

Library of Congress Cataloging in Publication Data

Houseman, Gerald L
  The right of mobility

  (National University publications) (Multi-disciplinary studies in the law)
  Bibliography: p.
  Includes index.
  1. Freedom of movement—United States.
I. Title.
KF4785.H68   342'.73'085   79-913
ISBN 0-8046-9239-4

To
PENNY

CONTENTS

FOREWORD

The right of mobility is not mentioned in the Constitution. Neither is the right to privacy, yet both are such essential elements of the human condition that they are recognized as basic rights in all post-feudal societies. They are in fact such fundamental concepts that they are generally taken for granted. Thus, when the Supreme Court was obliged to develop a constitutional foundation for the right of privacy in *Griswold v. Connecticut* (1965), Justice Douglas was forced to resort to "penumbras" emanating from the First, Third, Fourth, Fifth, and Ninth amendments. In fact, the marital privacy at issue in that case was, he said, "older than the Bill of Rights." Defending the right to travel in *Shapiro v. Thompson* (1969), Justice Stewart was forced to be equally devious, saying that there was no need "to ascribe the sources of the right . . . to a particular constitutional provision."

Mobility is so highly prized that its limitation is the principal sanction in all systems of criminal punishment. It is precisely because mobility is such a broad concept that it resists systematic study and analysis. It is closely related to many other values. Its exercise yields essential satisfactions but also creates difficult societal problems. For example, the automobile has provided mobility previously undreamed of to millions, while at the same time, at least in America, destroying systems of public transportation and leaving substantial numbers of citizens less mobile. But this is a minor concern compared with the impact this engine of mobility has had on world culture, environment, living patterns, morals, economy, and natural resources.

Gerald Houseman has bravely undertaken to write about mobility as a fundamental value, and to explore its contributions and its contradictions. He sees it as a necessary corollary to the full realization of all the freedoms listed in the Bill of Rights; and yet the concept itself is ill defined and relatively weak in American legal tradition and constitutional interpretation, however strong it may be in practice.

Old and new limitations on the right of mobility are now being confronted as public policy issues. Mobility problems of the crippled and handicapped are suddenly being realized, and across the nation street curbs have been broken to provide ramps for wheelchairs. At a much different level, the no-growth movement, through which numerous communities are endeavoring to preserve their character and avoid the costs and disruptions of population influx, is challenging traditional freedoms of movement and enterprise. Exclusionary zoning regulations, which have erected high walls of containment around privileged suburbs, are under attack in the courts and legislatures.

It is high time we began to think seriously about the benefits, the costs, and the paradoxes of mobility as a value, and about its practice in the all too real world. Houseman has done an invaluable service by posing these issues and beginning such a dialog.

C. Herman Pritchett

ACKNOWLEDGMENTS

The author is grateful to the National Endowment for the Humanities for its support through the award of a seminar-in-residence grant; to Indiana University at Fort Wayne for providing valuable sabbatical time to work on this project; to my colleagues in the NEH seminar at Santa Barbara, 1977-78; to Professor C. Herman Pritchett, who was very helpful in many ways; to Professor Philippa Strum of Brooklyn College, City University of New York, who was responsible for seeing that some of these ideas were publicly presented at the 1976 meeting of the American Political Science Association; and to Judy Violette, government documents librarian of Indiana University at Fort Wayne. Most of all, I am grateful to the members of my family for their encouragement and support.

THE RIGHT OF MOBILITY

ABOUT THE AUTHOR

Gerald L. Houseman is Associate Professor of Political Science at Indiana University in Fort Wayne, Indiana. He is the author of numerous articles in scholarly journals. His research interests center upon human rights questions in urban and industrial environments.

1

THE MOBILITY CRISIS

The right of mobility, a freedom as fundamental as free speech or privacy, is not recognized in the United States today in either de jure or de facto terms. The legal and constitutional position of the right of mobility rests neither upon the interstate commerce clause, the equal protection clause, nor the Bill of Rights. The right of travel, a right which does not extend to the broad parameters of the right of mobility, is possible only because the Supreme Court has said, in one instance, that there is a right to travel regardless of the absence of a specific constitutional provision and, in another instance, that people must accompany goods that are shipped in interstate commerce.[1]

These pronouncements seem merely an academic quibble to some of us when the de facto situation is surveyed. Look, for example, under the headline "In Suburbia 3 Cars May Not Be Enough":

[They] are one of the four out of a hundred American families who own three or more cars. Although to some people three cars may seem a mark of luxury and indulgence, to the B— [family] three cars represent a necessity, the only way to maintain freedom of action for each family member.

"Sometimes I think if we had four or five cars, we could probably use them," said Mrs. B—. With three sons approaching driving age, the thought is not wild speculation. "They're all talking about LTDs and Corvettes," she continued. . . . [*New York Times,* November 5, 1972]

There is no mobility problem, to say nothing of a "crisis," for this suburban family, and it is safe to assume that their perceptions are not unique. They are shared by many or most Americans in that large group which owns *less* than three cars.[2]

Mobility is clearly a problem and, much more than that, a crisis of unfathomable dimensions for many of the handicapped. Paralyzed from the neck down, a handicapped person contrasts the promise of the American dream with the hell of his reality:

The Declaration of Independence states that everyone has an inalienable right to life, liberty and the pursuit of happiness. Medical science has provided life, but where is liberty if I cannot cross the street because of a man-made barrier, the curb? How is my pursuit of happiness compatible with society's preoccupation with what I *cannot* do? And how can I pursue happiness if I am excluded from many of our society's normal social and recreational functions?[3]

This contrasts so glaringly with the three-car family that anyone might argue that setting out such extremes is an unfair way in which to proceed. Stark contrasts, all the same, demonstrate one form of reality, and they demonstrate it more graphically than the more conventional truism that the right of mobility appears to exist, albeit in the single mode of the automobile, for most Americans who are middle class, employed, white residents of the suburbs, and it exists not at all, or in a very limited form, for the poor, the black, the aged, the inner city resident, the rural tenant, and the physically limited (a term I prefer over "handicapped").

The purposes of this study are to examine why this is so, to look at newly developed critiques on the right of mobility, to array these critiques against the objective situation of lack of recognition of this right, to investigate the legal and constitutional possibilities of enforcement of this right, to look at the decision-making processes and structures which help to account for the disadvantaged position of the right of mobility, to define the right of mobility, and to posit some possible alternatives, including legislative remedies and even amendment of the Constitution.

These are difficult tasks. The right of mobility is a broad concept. Many of the issues which concern it have been with us for a long time—transportation, housing, taxation, land use and zoning, immigration and emigration, social welfare, industrial development, environmental protection—but they have generally been considered in isolation without reference to the public policy themes and unifying values which affect all of them. This requires retrieval and collation of types and quantities of information, much of it of a fugitive character, of such generality and vastness that it is well beyond the scope or ability of a single researcher or of a single study. A public or private agency staffed and equipped to monitor the progress, as well as the setbacks, in this important area of human rights will, it is to be hoped, come into existence at some future time, but it should now be considered only one of the potential developments created by this concern. In the meantime this study should be considered only a beginning effort and should not be expected to be in any way comprehensive. The development of public policy, and especially of the law, in this area adds to the problem because it is now in a state of flux. For example, new experiments in transportation, land use and zoning, housing, and environmental protection are now put forward on a constant and consistent basis. Legal developments—on no-growth community policies, on public housing sites in suburbia, on the school busing issue, on highway construction, and on a myriad of other concerns—are making daily additions to the literature on the right of mobility.

This research should go forward, all the same, since the right of mobility is a great, pressing, and relatively new concern of policy makers in all branches and at all levels of government. The breadth and importance of this right has never been fully appreciated. C. Herman Pritchett, the noted public law scholar, recently stated that the right of mobility is a constitutional problem of "wide-ranging scope," that scholars in the past have looked upon it only from the narrow perspective of the right of interstate travel, and that mobility is a right which "seems to rival privacy" in importance.[4]

This neglect of the right of mobility does not, however, mean that public policy and policy makers have left it unaffected. The automobile has been given leeway and preference at the expense of other possible modes of transport and at a high social cost borne by those who do not own or use cars.[5] Cheap FHA mortgages for low-density suburban housing have been encouraged at the expense of the inner city, at a profligate cost in energy resources, and have resulted in congestion which has harmed almost everyone's ability to go from here to there. Highways have been constructed, ironically in the name of mobility, which have temporarily eased the transportation problems of some while they have disrupted the mobility patterns, homes, neighborhoods, jobs, and lifestyles of others. Passports have been denied for trivial or vengeful reasons. Bus companies have been put out of business because of conspiracies fostered by General Motors. And those who are physically limited cannot lift their wheelchairs above curbings and cannot move from place to place within a single building because of untold obstacles and unwarranted thoughtlessness.

It can be argued that neglect of the right of mobility has even had a great deal to do with the physical appearance of America. Vaulting expressways, decaying city centers, and suburbs cluttered with little boxes all in a row on every cul-de-sac are hardly aesthetic visions. The "ghetto-ization" of this country that has resulted from the impacts of law and public policy must also be added to this list of woes, since the right of mobility must include social as well as physical mobility. Retirement communities and cheap downtown hotels are now the ghettos of the aged. Suburbs are for the young marrieds. The campuses and the military bases are for the young. The traditional ghettos and barrios are the homes of minorities. These trends have been strengthened through restrictive zoning practices, discrimination, auto-centered transportation systems, a general lack of effective land use planning, standards differentials in housing inspection, and, to a surprising extent, the development of environmental safeguards. This last factor has caused such groups as environmentalists and poverty workers to clash on questions of growth policy, industrial development, construction projects, and restrictions on certain types of land use.

The right of mobility, in short, faces a depressing landscape in both the literal and figurative sense. One traditional response to the inattention given this right is to charge policy makers with a skewed sense of values. Their interest-group approach to public policy making, according to this argument, has usually resulted in victories for special interests and in their enrichment at the expense of the public.[6] There appears to be more than ample evidence that this is the case, but recent research also shows that cost-benefit analysis and other supposedly "neutral" tools yield much the same kind of result.[7]

A different kind of response puts most of the blame on society and accounts for a lack of social conscience in public policy making because of the moral deficiencies of "the people." One cannot but be struck by the wrath and bitterness displayed by *New York Times* columnist Tom Wicker as he comments on the film *Nashville*. The movie, says Wicker, depicts the

> vulgarity, greed, deceit, cruelty, barely contained hysteria, and the frantic lack of root and grace into which American life has been driven by its own heedless vitality . . . the writhings of a culture that does not even know it is choking on exhaust fumes . . . a culture desperately clinging to the idea of value while vulgarizing almost every particular value . . . the American mobility culture, with its autos, obsolete and crunchable the day they're sold, its fastfood parlors, plastic motel rooms, take-out orders, transient sex and junk music.[8]

Mobility, as defined by Wicker, is almost a sin; at the very least it is a vulgar manifestation of overconsumption. But our concern is not mobility for the sake of mobility alone, which is what Wicker is alluding to, but mobility as a right that is denied to many people in many walks of life and social categories. Mobility is a right which makes many of the other rights we hold dear both tenable and possible—the rights of association, privacy, and equality of opportunity, for example. Enhancement of the right of mobility in this wholesome and dignified sense could even lead to a changed society in which the unhealthy tendencies deplored by Wicker become attenuated, less important, perhaps nearly eradicated. In the meantime it remains difficult to blame society, the people, for our ills, since a great deal of policy making—and this especially applies to mobility policy—has been carried out in an atmosphere of tenuous and even dubious connections with any mechanisms of popular consent.[9]

Still another response is the treatment of the right of mobility as an essentially technological question, and the usual response to technological developments has been to promote and encourage them. They laughed at Robert Fulton and his steamboat idea, we are told, but we have been laughing at such scoffers and skeptics ever since. There is, in addition to the technological assumption ("If you can do it, do it"), a powerful philosophy, symbolism, and mythology tied to such Western cultural ideals and traditions as progress, growth, and development. These have been charted well for us by writers such as Hannah Arendt, Herbert Marcuse, Jacques Ellul, Theodore Roszak, and Lewis Mumford.[10] All these may approach the technology issue with a different set of assumptions, but all of them decry, in one way or another, the hegemony of technology and of those who control the decisions which affect it. All these thinkers would be willing to say that, in one way or another, the right of mobility as well as other precious human rights have been sacrificed for the sake of the technological assumption. There must be some parting of company with the technological hegemony view, however, since resolution of the question of the right of mobility should be seen *primarily* as an issue of human will and imagination.

Human will can resolve that we shall resist technology and its innovations and development when it is felt that no good will come of it. There is some evidence that this is now happening; environmentalists, opponents of waste, those who argue for a reallocation of priorities, those who demand some accountability for governmental and corporate actions, and those who demand an enlargement of human freedom—women and minority groups, for example—all appear to be politically ascendant. All these groups are accelerating their actions and demands. If such diverse thinkers as Herbert Marcuse, Charles Reich, Alvin Toffler, and L. S. Stavrianos are correct, the days of prerogative for the sake of prerogative are numbered.[11] The demystification of hierarchy may be at hand. Human rights which have a fragile history or no history at all—such as equal rights for women—are being stridently demanded. People will no longer accept excuses, delays, lies, or the rationale of tradition—or of corporate profits—when these are seen as obstacles to their just needs and wants.

Though I have great sympathy with this hopeful point of view, I am sure that it must be tempered with caution, doubt, and even some defensive cynicism. Human will and its potential are not doubted; but an important underlying premise which tempers the approach of this book is the belief that the right of mobility is in its present state of underdevelopment because of misdirected human will. Like many needs—housing, education, aid to the cities, and income redistribution are good examples—it has been neglected and has suffered as a result of the loss of purpose and the squandering of resources on war, armaments, space, bureaucracy, and gross, stupefying consumerism and gadgetry which has taken up so much of the sixties and seventies. The right of mobility, then, is seen as a "priority politics" matter which should be neglected no longer.

If the optimistic observers listed above are correct, however, it then follows that the right of mobility is going to see a great day; for what is more basic or more important in human affairs? Repressive regimes have always known, and have invariably practiced, mobility control in order to ensure their own security and in order to maximize their exploitative potential. The intrinsic relationship between movement and personal freedom is verified by historical experience which ranges from feudalism to the contrasting conditions of black and white settlement in America, from Horatio Alger dreams of maximum mobility, social as well as physical, to the hopeless finality of Dachau.

The last response to the right of mobility issue which must be examined is that the mobility concept and the vast areas of public policy which it touches amount to what can be called the "defining of a non-problem into existence." Public policy has, after all, been developed, some of it very enlightened, to deal with each of the specific areas of concern which could be listed under the rubric of "mobility issues." This must be granted, but it appears to be equally correct to assert that the right of mobility, since it is such an all-embracing concept, provides the positive benefits of perceptual and conceptual unification of this vast variety of human concerns. In due time it appears likely to be demonstrated in a rigorously empirical fashion that such a unification will tend to lead to the discovery of the principles upon which such disparate issues as immigration, housing policy, anti-discrimination measures, and transport policy can dovetail, can be brought together to create an effective illustration of the kind of government and society that is needed. This looking at the whole forest rather than at one tree at a time is an approach that is endorsed by a host of empirical social scientists, by a variety of thinkers, and by policy makers. The purpose, of course, is not so much to aid in the practical and purposeful development of social science as to aid in the enlargement and promotion of human freedom. The neglect of the right of mobility and the attendant costs of this neglect have been brought about, in part, by a failure to note the effects of various kinds of policy making upon it. It is not "defining a non-problem into existence," furthermore, to be concerned about tendencies and problems that are writ large in a variety of public institutions, public policies, social issues, and human concerns.

My biases should be borne in mind as we proceed. I have a general preference for social change and a continuing belief, in these days of doubt, Zen, and lowered expectations, in human will. At the level of methods and tactics, I have an unashamed preference for the spirit of Quixote over that of Machiavelli.

2

MOBILITY
Concept and Definition

If the concept of mobility is so broad and all-embracing that it incorporates the right to passport ownership, welfare rights regardless of state of residence, transportation policy, immigration and emigration, job mobility, social mobility, and a host of other economic, social, and political considerations, how can the right of mobility be made workable as an instrument of law and public policy? How can it be defined? What is its relevance?

At the outset it must be acknowledged that adequate definition of the right of mobility is intimately bound up with its practical application. Law and public policy are incapable of application if they are undefinable, and too many political conflicts are based upon this first cause. Definition is therefore a precondition both for the ultimate goal of establishing this right firmly as a fixture of law and public policy and for the purpose of clarity as we move along the path towards this goal.

The transcendent reason for establishing the right of mobility is to prevent abuses of human freedom, whether these are threatened by governments, private persons or institutions, or agents of one sort or another. The right of mobility must become a civil right. But this, unfortunately, is not enough in itself to ensure the right to mobility. Roger Nett, a scholar who has written about human rights and who has studied the right of mobility from the standpoint of a philosopher, tells why:

... it takes little examination to see that to call something a civil right is to use more than a legal concept. Legality is only a small part of it. We do not say, for example, that people who are enslaved, where slavery is legal, are enjoying basic human rights; rather, we say the opposite, that such rights are being forgone. Law does not define right. . . .[1]

The right of mobility, then, has a justification which goes well beyond legal considerations. It is a recognized social "good," a first premise, that people should possess a right of mobility in order to realize the best approximation of their hopes and desires, and also in order to escape those persons or forces which may threaten their existence, their livelihood, their culture, their loved ones, or their human rights, including the right of mobility. If rights were not conceived apart from law, there would have been no Magna Carta, no French Revolution, no Declaration of Independence.[2]

The moral basis of the right of mobility is best put in succinct terms by Ivan Illich:

People are born almost equally mobile. Their natural mobility speaks for the personal liberty of each to go where he or she wants. Equity demands the protection of this right against any abridgment. For the sake of this protection it is irrelevant to ask by which means a person's mobility is threatened: by imprisonment, by bondage to an estate, by revoking his passport, or by enclosing him within an environment that encroaches upon his mobility in order to make him a consumer of transport.[3]

The process of transferring a moral concept into law and public policy, however, is fraught with analytical and logical problems and dilemmas, with practical problems of application, with the obstacles of customs and mores (is Illich saying, for example, that all prisoners should be set free?), and with the problem of the inertia which is built into our legal system, requiring that rights be demanded before they can be granted.

It can also be persuasively argued that the law has generally represented the interests of the rulers, the elites, and the governing establishments of most societies. The law therefore is more often than not a conservatizing force, a force which prevents the expression, and certainly the expansion, of human rights. The civil rights movements of recent years often found the forces of the law arrayed against them even though they were working in consonance, in their own eyes at least, with lawful purposes. Elites and governing establishments will use every instrument at their disposal against the achievement of positive social, economic, and political gains, including racism, intimidation, repression, custom, and tradition. The latter was often used against the civil rights movement in both the North and the South, and the advocates of the Equal Rights Amendment have found this to be one of the most effective weapons against their cause. Those who seek to expand human freedoms must be iconoclasts. No other way is usually open to them. If the law does occasionally serve them with justice, it may be merely coincidence or it may be that the time has come for acceptance of a new idea.

The numerous problems of transferring the right of mobility from a moral to a legal concept help to account for the failure to develop it to a position comparable to that of such rights as privacy or free speech, but it is also probable that ruling elites, in a great variety of times and places, have discouraged its development. The sharecropping system in the South, for example, depended upon an immobility close to that of pre-Civil War days and prevented mobility through a constant and growing burden of indebtedness. Coalminers of Kentucky and West Virginia, among other places, have lived in fenced-off compounds of company housing and have had to do their shopping at the company store. Residents of nursing homes are often faced with prison-like strictures, and they have the certain knowledge that escape will confront them with such dangers as hunger and exposure.

Immobility is strongly rooted in an important historical basis. One of the great advantages of American life, until now at least, has traditionally been our ability to pull up stakes and leave for more favorable climes when faced with adversity or lack of opportunity. America has also served—its history of slavery and indentured settlement notwithstanding—as a refuge from European and Asian despotisms, class rigidities, and starvation. Before the American experience, however, the right of mobility had a much less bright history. The laws, customs, and traditions of feudalism militated strongly against mobility. The right of mobility was generally unavailable to all except the rulers and ruling classes. For Jews movement and settlement eventually were limited to those areas of the city (since land ownership was forbidden) marked by the boundaries of ghetto walls; this restriction was in addition to limitations to certain sections of the country—the "pale"—as well as limitations upon the types of occupations, livelihoods, and homes that could be maintained.

Industrialization of Europe brought movements of people from rural areas to towns, but it took considerable periods of time before an appreciable rise in living standards and, more to the point, it took until the late nineteenth and early twentieth centuries before such basic rights as the vote were accorded to the working classes. The right of mobility was severely limited for centuries before it found expression in some modern constitutions and in the great migrations to America, Australia, and other parts of the world. The right of mobility has therefore had a rather dismal history, at least until the past one or two centuries, and it still faces great problems to the present day. In England, for example, it is often impossible to move to smaller towns unless you can show both an ability to earn an income there, usually through employment with a local firm, and advance provision for living quarters. Local firms, of course, generally prefer local people for employment. The absence of rental or purchase property, job opportunities, or building permits—any one of these three—will prevent in-migration to smaller towns. Now American towns are setting up similar obstacles, usually citing environmental reasons, against the right of mobility.[4] The traditions of a less mobile Europe may be catching up with us now that America is largely settled and developed and its frontier, both in a physical and a psychological sense, has disappeared.

The history of the right of mobility demonstrates that any definition of this right must link physical with social mobility, not only because of the obvious preconditions set by the former upon the latter but also because strong evidence suggests that both physical and social mobility are long-accepted elements of the American value system; in other words, the American people demand mobility. Part of the American love affair with the automobile amounts to this, and the overly maligned Turner thesis of the American frontier and of the westering impulse appears to be verified by the social and cultural values and experience of the nation. Recent studies of urban settlement and development show further that, contrary to the generally accepted Chicago School of sociology view which held that a causal relationship existed between residential "instability" and urban pathology, there is strong evidence that "impermanent" urban groups have tended to fit the generally accepted definitions of "solid citizenship"—middle classness, upward mobility patterns, and so forth—more than those who have lived in stability (permanent or semi-permanent) neighborhoods. The impermanent groups even tended to vote in greater numbers than the stability neighborhoods did.[5] It is interesting, though not too important for our purposes, that this tends to undermine some of the assumptions made about neighborhoods by popular writers such as Jane Jacobs, Alvin Toffler, and Daniel P. Moynihan.

One cannot become too concerned with stability, instability, or solid citizenship, however, in assessing the place of the right of mobility in America's history, culture, and values. It will suffice to point out, for present purposes, that even without regard for the importance of this value in American culture and mythology, there appears to be a common sense preference for a life of movement and, with it, a life of variety, and that this preference is strong enough to win support among social scientists, policy makers, and social theorists while disturbing some of the critics of popular culture.[6]

The place of mobility as a value can also be defined by looking at contrasting images such as nursing homes, suburban subdivisions, and retirement communities. (Prisons or other places of totally involuntary confinement do not, of course, lend themselves to fair comparisons.) It may be objected that the right of mobility cannot be analyzed in the light of such phenomena as nursing homes, suburban tracts, or retirement communities because these are, in the main, voluntary arrangements that have been entered into under no compulsion. This argument is specious, since it assumes (1) that these represent real choices; most of us are usually faced with a rather narrow set of choices about what type of community we can pick to live in; (2) that individual satisfaction and self-fulfillment are attainable in an environment marked by conformity, sameness, and discrimination practiced against those who might enter the community and upset its perceptions of what it should be like; and (3) that a choice of community may on many occasions be a permanent and unalterable yet untenable decision of most unfortunate consequences. The literature on retirement communities, for example, tends to offer depressing reports of conformity, apathy, and joylessness, and it seems reasonable to assume that these can be traced to feelings of isolation and immobility.[7] Suburban development has generally been shaped by land use and loan policies, racial discrimination, the special interests of banks and speculators, differentials in enforcement of codes and inspection standards, and highway policies and expenditures.[8] Public policy will never be able to achieve relief for every individual who finds himself or herself in such isolated and confined circumstances, but a great deal can be done to promote diversity, non-discrimination, and retrieval of unfortunate gambles or bad bargains. The right of mobility will be enhanced to the extent that these are achieved.

Mobility is much more, however, than the amelioration of feelings of isolation or the negatively stated right of non-confinement. It must also be defined as a process, and this is important because most mobility involves a destination. It is possible to conceive of a number of situations in which the right of mobility may be exercised with no particular goal or destination in mind: one may just want to travel until he or she finds a satisfying place in which to locate, one may go on a journey with no particular end in mind, or one may just go out for a walk. In these limited instances the definition of mobility as a process may not be important. Most movement is carried out, however, with a destination in mind, and in these instances the right of mobility must include both movement and the right of peaceful settlement at the point of destination. Recent court decisions dealing with zoning restrictions, construction of low-cost public housing in suburban neighborhoods, and the movement of children from inner city to suburban schools in order to achieve equality in education have in each case had to deal with the concept of the right of mobility in this way.[9] A variety of other needs—the protection of squatters' rights, rights against extradition in a number of circumstances, and quite obviously, the right to privacy—may depend upon an understanding of the right of mobility as a process. Mobility as a process is therefore a vital element in defining this right.

It follows that the right of mobility is not absolute. A host of considerations relating to private property ownership, tenants' rights, safety, security, environmental considerations, the right to privacy, the protections against unlawful search and seizure, the preservation of historic buildings and monuments, academic freedom, and public health policies could be invoked, in certain times and places, against one's mobility. The abuse or overuse of governmental power against the right of mobility in the past does not vitiate legitimate employment of such power in the public interest. The exercise of the right of mobility, then, can be made subject to the facts and circumstances which surround such exercise. This appears to be borne out by the various constitutions which do recognize a right of mobility or movement of some kind, for in all but one of these, the UN Universal Declaration of Human Rights, it is made clear that the right of mobility is not absolute.[10] Much of the problem of non-recognition of the right of mobility may in fact stem from procedural considerations. There are few, if any, presumptions written into American law, for example, which favor or which presume a right of mobility.

The juxtaposition of the right of mobility and other human rights also makes it clear that most of the other rights we hold dear are dependent upon a well-recognized right of mobility. Perhaps the most direct connections can be made with the right of association, the Fourteenth Amendment right to equal protection, the due process demanded by the Bill of Rights, and the habeas corpus right against unlawful detention. It is not difficult, however, to recall or imagine a variety of circumstances in which the right of mobility could be linked with any of the other important human rights recognized in the Constitution and in the law—free speech, freedom of religion, freedom against cruel and unusual punishments, or the right to a fair trial in a venue expected to produce a fair result. The right of mobility was the subject of a complex of issues, it should be noted, during the great civil rights struggles of the late fifties and throughout the sixties. The bus boycott in Montgomery, Alabama, in 1957 under the leadership of Martin Luther King, Jr., the freedom riders and the movement to desegregate buses and terminals in the early sixties, and the fight over public accommodations and the applicability of the interstate commerce clause were all issues of mobility in a direct sense. All the great civil rights struggles of course involved social mobility and the enlargement of human rights. The right of mobility is therefore not just a frill or flourish to be added to the Constitution and/or legal precedent: it is a necessary corollary to full recognition of all of the freedoms listed in the Bill of Rights and supported by law, custom, and tradition.

Neither the constitutional nor the legal position of the right of mobility in America is clear, however, despite occasional lip service which this principle receives from the bench and despite the development of support for it in the Universal Declaration of Human Rights and a number of national constitutions.[11] On the other hand, it can be shown that more than an occasional proposal is made to limit mobility severely, leaving open the possibility that the few strands of support this idea has managed to muster over the years could be swept away. A number of proposals offered in the 95th Congress carry dangerous portents. One bill, for example, would establish a system of "forgery-proof" Social Security cards, complete with photograph and plastic lamination, for everyone entitled to have one; the ostensible purpose is to control the flow of illegal immigration into the country.[12] Though its sponsors deny the possibility that this could easily be turned into a national identification system, it is not difficult to imagine this being done in the name of bureaucratic efficiency, national security, or, if the recent history of the FBI and the CIA are any guide, just in order to snoop and perhaps to limit mobility. Internal passports are the hallmark of repressive regimes such as South Africa, the Soviet Union, or Nazi Germany.

The domestic passport idea, moreover, has just recently been rejected by the Federal Advisory Committee on False Identification. Former Assistant Attorney General Richard Thornburgh, who was deeply involved with the work of the committee, said at the conclusion of its work that "that type of solution has 1984 overtones."[13] The advocates of this approach, however, are pressing on with their claims that this will effectively block illegal immigration and fraudulent identification.

Edward C. Banfield, a well-known urban affairs expert, proposes confinement to small, remote towns and areas for individuals who, though they may have committed no crime, can be shown through a series of statistical indices to be *likely* to become criminals. This "Banfield banishment" is found in a list of proposed solutions to urban problems in the eighth and tenth chapters of *The Unheavenly City* and of the revised work *The Unheavenly City Revisited.*[14]

Offensive and ill-considered proposals such as Banfield's and the domestic passport tend to crop up over and over again because of their ideological basis—rightist or far rightist—or, even more likely, because some efficiency-minded bureaucrat or foundation researcher has decided that these are in our interest. The right of mobility must be considered weak and endangered. For some groups in American society, such as the elderly or the physically limited, it barely exists at all. For those to whom this right has occasionally been applied, as in the *Passport Cases,* there appears to be no constitutional source which the Supreme Court has been willing to enunciate with any clarity or consistency.[15] There is, in other words, no clear body of law and no clear mandate of the Constitution which can be relied upon to support a right of mobility as set out here: one which links social and physical mobility and protects both, which protects individuals in a status of less than total confinement, which is viewed as a process both of movement and of settlement, which helps to protect other important provisions of the Bill of Rights and the Constitution, and which guarantees and permits a right of movement in the absence of other important or conflicting sets of fact and circumstance, such as the protection of some other human right.

This is not a totally satisfying definition of the right of mobility, but it appears to be a practical set of characterizations which can lead to its use as a workable instrument of law and public policy. The only important missing ingredient in this definition which prevents workability, or practical application, of this right is a legal and policy *presumption* in favor of mobility. A list of considerations which qualify the right of mobility was set out above; other valid qualifiers could be added to this list, but once these are drawn together—and what they amount to, really, are some generally accepted standards of human behavior—it is then possible to say that in the absence of such qualifiers there should be a presumption in law and public policy in favor of the free movement of persons over any part of the· country and, perhaps one day, over any part of the earth.[16]

This presumption should be stated legislatively and constitutionally (a formal amendment of the Constitution may even be necessary), it should be given support by public administration practitioners, and it should be both a procedural and substantive component of the law.[17] Not even these broad mandates should be permitted to limit the right of mobility, for it is quite valid, indeed highly desirable, that the qualifications imposed upon this right should be frequently reviewed. This goes on at the present time on a compartmentalized, issue-by-issue basis: zoning restrictions and practices are questioned, the institutionalization of people is coming under attack on an increasing basis, Jessica Mitford and Swedish government officials question the need for prisons, and auto-centered transport systems have led to second thoughts. Strong public policy support of the right of mobility as a set approach to a broad band of social issues could lead to enlargement of this right if there is a recognition of its breadth of application.

A public policy assumption in favor of the right of mobility would undoubtedly lead as well to mitigation, and in time perhaps eradication, of the effects of narrow choices of residence that have been brought about by the ghetto-ization of America. The enclaves of the elderly, the suburbanites, the minorities, and other groups could become open to diversity and a new sense of freedom, and the lie would be given to the "voluntarism" alleged for these associations and choices. All this is a long way off. In the meantime there remain the essential tasks of sharpening the definition of mobility, developing the aims of mobility as a concept and as a right, and promoting the adoption of its presumption in public policy matters.

At the present time there is no consensus on the desirability of the right of mobility. There are qualms about the further promotion of a "mobile society." There are even wide disagreements over whether mobility can be adequately defined, or if it can, whether it really describes the social focus necessary for the expansion of human freedom and the prudent application of policy. For example:

"Mobility" is not an easy concept to define. In ordinary parlance, it usually refers to the ease with which a person can move about or the amount of movement he performs. But what is important is not movement as such; it is *access to people and facilities*. Access, not movement, is the true aim of transport. One may have access to facilities without moving much at all. An immobile person may have water and gas at the flick of a switch, have his refuse collected, receive calls from his doctor, and deliveries from the shops, be informed and entertained by wireless and television, talk to his friends on the telephone, all without stirring from his house. In a well endowed town a person may have access to a vast range of facilities with very little travelling. While possibly less mobile in the ordinary sense of the word than someone who travels greater distances to work, school and recreation or to visit friends, he may nevertheless be better placed, since the act of travel, with the time, cost, and personal effort involved, is something which he usually would prefer to avoid.[18]

"Access" is sometimes a handy term to use in discussions of mobility or mobility-related issues, and it is quite popular among transport-conscious and environmentally oriented writers.[19] The term is not a good substitute for "mobility," however, for it refers only to a limited number of circumstances in which access may be operative in place of physical mobility. Since the right of mobility refers to social as well as physical mobility, as well as to their interdependence, the term has obvious inadequacies. But it is not even a good substitute for physical mobility, for it describes something *other* than mobility. In many cases, as outlined above, it describes immobility. It can even mean, apparently without consultation with immobile persons, an assumption of the undesirability of a right of mobility for them. This seems mean-spirited, because we are a long way from the time when choices about mobility can actually be made by the elderly, the physically limited, and other groups. The adoption of access as a social goal in place of mobility may at first blush appear to be a broader and more useful approach, but the most cursory examination shows that this is deceptive.

"Travel" is also inadequate as a substitute for mobility. Again we have a term which can refer only to physical mobility, though of course it can lead to the enhancement of social mobility. The right to travel has received some significant support in court precedents, particularly in some interpretations of the Fifth Amendment, and some of this support comes from recognition that physical mobility is tied up with social mobility, as in *Shapiro v. Thompson.*[20] "Travel," unlike mobility, is a term one can find in the law dictionaries. The legal position of the right to travel can be of great assistance in development of the right of mobility; but it is not synonymous. It is instead a part of the many sets of considerations (though admittedly a vital part) which together provide a concept of the right of mobility.

"Access" and "travel" are therefore rejected, for several good reasons, as substitutes for "mobility." It is possible that an adequate substitute could be found which might do a better job of promoting this social goal. "Mobility" will perform this task for the time being.

3

THE LEGAL AND CONSTITUTIONAL
POSITION OF THE
RIGHT OF MOBILITY

Mobility has always been taken for granted by most Americans. The entire historical experience of the nation has been affected, strongly and directly, by the continuous migration and movement patterns that are now reflected in the country's demography. The familiar history and stories of migration from Europe and from other continents, of settlement in America, and later of movement to the West are important elements of our culture and traditions. Movement and resettlement continue to manifest themselves to such an extent that America is still the most mobile society in the world. The right of mobility issue, on appearance, would seem to be moot.

Two countervailing trends, both of which have been in evidence for some time, are nevertheless operating against the present and future exercise of this right. In addition, both these trends are getting stronger by the year. The first of these is the growth of technology and the assumptions which lie behind this growth; the second is the closing of the frontier.

The growth of technology, especially in electronics, has made it possible as never before to keep track of people and their movements. The right of privacy has been imperiled by these developments, and the recently exposed conduct of the FBI, the CIA, Internal Revenue, the White House, and a myriad of national, state, and local government agencies—as well as of corporate giants such as General Motors and American Telephone and Telegraph—has given rise to anxious concerns of civil libertarians, constitutional scholars, and some of the general public.[1] The right of privacy, however threatened, still has many friends and supporters; the literature on privacy demonstrates this in both quantitative and qualitative measures. The right of mobility, however, has not received the same attention, and much of this lapse can be explained only by an apathy and indifference born out of the great American traditions and experience of mobility. In the meantime there is growing evidence of technological capability in the task of keeping track of everyone: the states cooperate more closely in records maintenance on such matters as traffic violations, for example, or a proposal is made to link internal security data of Canada and the United States in one bank of information, or some fine bureaucrat proposes that as many personal documents as possible—bank account numbers, credit cards, medical records, drivers' licenses, employment files, or whatever—be given the same number, usually the Social Security number. Movement, anonymity, and the ability to change one's identity or occupation have become more difficult than in the past, and the outlook is not encouraging.

The closing of the American frontier has also resulted in the restriction of movement. This closing is not necessarily the one which might be associated with the sale of the last parcel of land in California or Alaska, but is rather a psychological phenomenon as much as it is physical. It is related to the completion of land development and settlement in large tracts of the West and of the Sun Belt and to a general awareness of this completion, but it is also related to feelings of the American people: feelings which include a revolt against technology, bigness, and institutions of most kinds, feelings which often reflect a distaste for urban life and a belief in resuscitation of the environment, and feelings which are motivated by altruism as well as by self-centeredness.[2] People now seek out small towns, remote places, or rural cooperatives and move into them; this is a reversal of the urbanization trend that has existed since the founding of the country. These places become their last frontier. People also realize that there is now a much greater shortage of quiet and unspoiled places and they are willing to pay premium prices and readjust career patterns and lifestyles in order to live in these places.[3] The closing of the frontier, then, is a closing off of opportunity, for that has been the historical importance and promise of the frontier. This closing becomes ever more apparent as those who obtain these last few desirable places work to keep others out of them through a variety of zoning and environmental restrictions.

The frontier serves well as a device for conceptualizing the freedom of movement issue. The frontier, after all, continues in the national consciousness of America as a symbol of an important spatial dimension of human freedom, hope, and opportunity.[4] Most importantly, the frontier has represented a unique break with the past, the European experience of immobility, social and physical, which characterizes much of the history of Western civilization. The centuries-old traditions of feudalism and caste were dominant over perhaps all but the past two hundred years of Western experience.

Immobility was the pattern of life preferred for the masses by those who dominated them. Spain, for example, required a license to travel of any individual crossing the Atlantic in either direction.[5] Imperial Russia often prevented letters, especially those containing exhortations to leave, from arriving at the homes of potential migrants. The English government's system of poor relief, established in 1601, tied the benefits of any such relief, as well as employment itself, to local residency.[6] Tyrants long have recognized that physical and social immobility go hand in hand, for it is almost impossible to obtain one of these without the other.

American law also generally recognizes this principle. Although American law in this field has tended to concern itself with the right of travel as opposed to a more generalized right of social and physical mobility, there is some evidence which demonstrates that judges, legal scholars, and certain precedents recognize the implicit connection between physical and social mobility. Even those decisions which have set back the cause of mobility, such as the Supreme Court's recent holding on high-density housing proscriptions, recognize this connection.[7]

It should therefore be asked whether public policy should be formulated with a unified concept of mobility in mind, one which includes social as well as physical aspects. Though the answer may seem obviously affirmative, it is clear that this has not been done, since there is no de jure recognition of a right of mobility in America. Most unfortunately, it seems equally clear that this is not likely to occur in the near future. The inert nature of Congress and of governmental processes generally, the special disadvantages borne by any innovation, and the attitudes and make-up of the Burger Court all point in a discouraging direction. To understand why this is the case, it is necessary to look at developments to date in law and public policy, to analyze the political factors which emerge from these developments, and to explore some of the advantages which could be gained by this unified—social and physical—conception of the right of mobility. In favor of this unified conception it can be shown (1) that there is some historical basis for it, (2) that its absence from consideration and a number of court decisions point to the need for reestablishing this right in the law in the form of a unified conceptualization, (3) that discussions of the right of travel by legal scholars often point up the need, from a law and public policy standpoint, to develop this unified approach to mobility, and (4) that a right of movement is recognized in a number of constitutions and legal contexts on an international basis, and this right is supported in the literature of philosophy, ethics, and law.

There can be little doubt as to the general state of confusion in the law of the right of travel. The right of travel is of course considerably less broad than the right of movement, both conceptually as well as in application, and this is especially so when social mobility is included in the latter. It is a necessary starting point, however, since it touches most closely upon the right of mobility. Incidentally, there appears to be little which distinguishes "mobility" and "movement," and the terms appear to be interchangeable to a very considerable degree.

The patent awarded to Sir Humphrey Gilbert, the first would-be English colonizer, by Elizabeth I in 1578 set the pattern for the charters of Virginia, Massachusetts Bay, Georgia, and the other original colonies:

And we doe geve full aucthoritie and power to the said Sir Humfrey that he shall and maye at all and every tyme and tymes hereafter have take and leade in the said voyages to travell thetherward or to inhabite there with him such and soe many of our subjects as shall willingely accompany him with sufficient shippinge and furnyture for their transportacions Soe that none of the same parsons be such as hereafter shalbe specially restrayned by us our heirs or successors. . . .[8]

This is a clear assurance of freedom of movement. Moreover, there had been a long-standing precedent for this, going back as far as the Magna Carta, which guaranteed free passage into and out of the realm.[9] Much later Blackstone's *Commentaries* set out a right to travel which seems to include support for social as well as physical mobility: "The personal liberty consists in the power of locomotion, of changing situation, or moving one's person to whatsoever place one's own inclination may direct, without imprisonment or restraint, unless by due process of law."[10] The right to travel between the colonies was generally recognized, and the Articles of Confederation guaranteed that the "people of each state shall have free ingress and regress to and from any other state."[11] There is no specific right to travel in the U.S. Constitution, however, and we have nothing stronger than surmise to explain this omission. The most likely reason, it seems to be agreed, is that it was taken for granted that the right to travel existed.

The unified conceptualization of social as well as physical mobility appears to have some historical basis in the colonial charters, Sir Humphrey Gilbert's patent being typical in its language, terms, and mandate, and in Blackstone's *Commentaries* where the clause "of changing situation" and the clause "one's own inclination" seem to point to something more than mere physical movement. The Articles of Confederation are quite clearly limited to physical movement, however, since the free ingress clause excepts "paupers, vagabonds and fugitives from justice."[12] The Articles notwithstanding, it nonetheless seems clear that the joining of social and physical mobility have been with us for a long time, as the other two examples attest. This long-standing recognition of the need to develop the idea of movement in concurrent social and physical terms can occasionally be found in the literature of law and public policy. It cannot be argued that this has consistently been done, for the Articles and many other examples stand against that proposition, but it has often been done, and the mere fact of this accomplishment so long ago is quite amazing in light of the dismal history of the right of mobility.

It remains difficult to see how this unified conceptualization of the right of movement can make any progress so long as American law continues to be in a state of confusion on the right to travel, the more elementary question which has nevertheless impeded development of this unification. The right to travel is well recognized in a welter of court decisions, but there has been a strong reluctance to attach it to any provision of the Constitution.[13] At various times it has found support in the privileges and immunities clause of article 4, section 2, in the privileges or immunities clause of the Fourteenth Amendment, in the "penumbra" of the First Amendment, in the due process clause of the Fifth Amendment, and in the commerce clause.[14] This last source has been said to recognize that people are needed to accompany goods that are transported interstate.[15] More recently the Supreme Court has been content to assure us that the right to travel is a generally established human right long supported by national practice which needs no particular reference point in the Constitution.[16] Despite this assurance there has been support in the past, and in the not-too-distant past, given by the Court to blatant abuses of the right to travel.[17]

It could be argued that the reluctance of the Court to tie the right to travel to a specific provision is justified on the grounds that, first, no specific provision does in fact exist, and second, judicial inflexibility on the question could be induced by insistence upon reference to a provision. The cases to date demonstrate an enormous variety of surrounding facts and circumstances ranging from airline regulation to qualifications for admission to a publicly owned hospital, and it could be that a rigid definition of the right to travel would yield a great deal of unnecessary litigation.[18] The right to travel has been successfully invoked, moreover, in a diversity of important causes such as voting rights, the search for employment, health care benefits, and housing.[19]

Criticism remains. Advocates of the right to travel have taken the courts to task:

... the right to travel is still in its infancy. While the Supreme Court makes sweeping statements about the extent and protection of the right, many state and lower federal courts are reluctant to accept the right to travel as a fundamental right. ...[20]

... the Court has bypassed the thorny problem of grounding freedom of travel in specific constitutional language and has proceeded to build an elaborate judicial construct on an exceptionally vague and uncertain foundation.[21]

Some of these same critics, however, are sufficiently heartened by the tenor and thrust of such decisions as *Shapiro v. Thompson* (1969) to ask whether the Court may develop the right to travel "to its logical conclusion ... the destruction of state boundaries and a guarantee of free movement for all citizens."[22] Though this does not appear likely in the near future, this concern underlines the incompleteness of the law on the right to travel, and it points to something *more* than the development of the right to travel. A variety of recent court decisions and legal scholars have connected the right to travel, expressly or impliedly, with a broader conceptualization of the right of movement, which describes social as well as merely physical mobility. This is not exactly a new legal frontier; Blackstone, as we have seen, tended to equate the right of movement with liberty itself. Nonetheless, it is a departure from the recent past, especially within the context of American law.

Shapiro v. Thompson may best fit the rubric of the right to travel cases, but it also suggests a unified conceptualization of social and physical mobility by its elimination of certain state residence requirements in welfare administration.[23] Similarly, *Memorial Hospital v. Maricopa County* (1974) found the fundamental right to travel compromised in an "impinging" manner when health care benefits were denied to a new settler in the state.[24] *Dunn v. Blumstein* (1972) struck a blow for voting rights as well as movement when state-imposed durational residence requirements for voting were found to be a "penalty" placed upon these fundamental rights. Again a deterring effect upon travel had been found to have been placed upon those exercising this right.[25] However, the Court has also denied certiorari to an argument invoking the right to travel against no-growth or slow-growth zoning laws.[26]

These tendencies and suggestions do not amount to a consistent development of the law towards a generally recognized right of movement. Indeed it can be argued that such decisions as *Sosna v. Iowa* (1975) and *Lawrence v. Oakes* (1973) represent a retreat from the doctrines of *Shapiro* and similar cases.[27] In *Sosna* Justice William Rehnquist found that state residency requirements for obtaining a divorce were sufficiently justified by state interests. In *Lawrence v. Oakes* the refusal of a local community to participate in a federal housing program was found not to be violative of the right to travel of migrants and potential migrants who would face employment disadvantages since they could not be housed locally.

Two cases, *In re May Barcomb* and *Shavers v. Kelly* (both 1974), point up particularly well the dilemmas of public policy on the right of movement.[28] In the first case unemployment benefits were denied to an applicant who left her job because she had no car and no way to get to her job. Though the court agreed that the right to travel may be an intrastate as well as interstate right, it held the denial of benefits to be only incidentally based upon her lack of transportation.[29] In *Shavers v. Kelly* it was alleged that Michigan's no-fault insurance law, by requiring expensive premiums, resulted in indigents' loss of the right to travel. Indigents cannot afford this insurance even though automobile travel is often the only means of transport available in the state. The court found that although the premiums were expensive and although automobiles are often the only practical transport mode and the mandatory nature of the insurance law would cause the poor to give up their cars, the right to travel had not been infringed because there is "no express legislative purpose to burden the right to travel."[30]

The effect of these decisions is to require car ownership and use by any and all persons who wish to exercise a right of movement on a level of some kind of equality with others. May Barcomb was required to own, or at least have use of, a car in order to enjoy all the benefits of employment, including employment itself. The *Shavers* decision requires, impliedly though not expressly, car ownership in order to enjoy the right of movement at all. Both propositions are outrageous in an age of energy crisis, environmental awareness, and respect for the principle of equality. Movement, rather than a mere right to travel, is operative in both cases, since both imply and relate to the unified conceptualization—social as well as physical—of movement in a most direct way. If, for example, the strict equal protection test advocated by Justice Marshall in his dissent in *Village of Belle Terre v. Boraas*[31] (1974) had been applied to these cases, state laws and practices (and perhaps some federal ones as well) could be strongly challenged by public interest lawyers:

... the reality facing many urban residents is that if one does not own a car, one has no means of reaching shopping areas, church, work, or medical facilities. Many industries have moved miles outside the city and, as a consequence, they are far from the reach of public transportation. Is not the right of these urban residents to travel denied when they cannot afford a car to reach these necessities? Yet the state provides funds for highways only and not for public transportation facilities. The state practice of ignoring public transportation and funding only highways ... impinges on the right to travel of those persons who ... cannot (economically or actually) afford a car.[32]

This is more than a right to travel matter, however, for "the right to travel is a personal freedom of liberty of movement."[33] Legal scholars aver this, sometimes even unwittingly, when they say that mobility is liberty itself[34] or when they assert that "the nature and constitutional source of the right to travel are not merely interesting academic puzzles. These issues must be resolved by the Supreme Court *if the full potential of the freedom of mobility concept is to be realized.* . . ."[35]

Marshall's equal protection test can also be applied to a great variety of facts and circumstances other than those of the automobile—to state and local statutes and ordinances which deny rights of movement, settlement, housing, land uses, health and welfare benefits, voting, job opportunities, and education. An equal protection argument against the *effects,* as distinguished from overt discriminatory policies, of zoning laws and growth restrictions is also conceivable. Unfortunately, a situation exists in which neither the equal protection clause nor the privileges and immunities clauses nor any constitutional provision has proved to be an adequate basis for the formulation of a doctrine of the right of movement. Perhaps a constitutional amendment is in order.[36] Such a guideline, whether it be an amendment, a statute, or a court decision, would also have to take into account the possible abuses of a right of movement, which cannot be an absolute right. One possible guideline was set out in *Cole v. Housing Authority* (1970) which may prove to be helpful: strict scrutiny of a law is to be involved only when a law penalizes migration, that is, travel with intent to settle, not when it penalizes simple transience.[37] This obviously does not go far enough; a whole set of guidelines must be devised to provide, for example, for the physically limited, the elderly, the users of public transportation, and the carless. This would only be a beginning towards a generally-recognized right of mobility.

Law does not define rights in any case, and this can be seen in the occasional, or more than occasional, proposals which are brought forward to limit mobility severely—no-growth statutes, population limits, domestic passports, work cards which could also double as passes under a national system of mobility control. Changes in law and public policy can, all the same, help to promote positive attitudes, even on the part of government officials, towards the right of mobility, and can aid in establishing a climate that is responsive to this right.

4

THE DE FACTO POSITION OF
MOBILITY IN AMERICAN SOCIETY

In many respects the legal and constitutional position of the right of mobility defines the policy position, the de facto position, of this right. If the issue of mobility in present-day American society is to be measured with any completeness, however, it is necessary to look at some factors and developments which may or may not be the subject of any legislation or case law now on the books. The overwhelming thrust of technological developments, combining with the social phenomenon of the closing of the frontier, has brought us to an absurd and alarming point at which mobility is threatened in this country as never before and in which, ironically, our valid and often noble concern with aesthetic and environmental considerations has brought on an overreaction which could be fatal to our mobile traditions.

Technological developments can of course enhance mobility, but many of them have served as anti-mobility forces bringing about low-density and energy-wasteful urban growth patterns, dependence upon the automobile as the single transport mode in most locations, bureaucratic preferences for electronic data banks and border patrol devices, and a host of other innovations; all these are commonly perceived as a kind of progress which, some would say, should not be resisted and in fact cannot be resisted.

There is resistance, anyway, for a variety of causes, and new awarenesses—environmental, consumerist, aesthetic, anti-capitalist, communalist, and sometimes religious—have lent support to a strident anti-technology feeling in our national consciousness which has arisen out of well-founded doubts about the automobile, nuclear energy, processed foods, economic growth in the traditional sense of the term, population growth, and a great variety of governmental and corporate policies and practices. This reaction to the traditional technological assumption—that if you can do it technologically it is ipso facto desirable socially—must be commended. The Naderites, the "whistle blowers" in industry, government, and such specialties as nuclear engineering, the supporters of the late E. F. Schumacher and his *Small Is Beautiful* ideas, the commune experimenters, the Zen philosophers, the Zero Population Growth and Zero Automobile Growth people, the conservationists working with solar energy, windmills, and energy-saving structural designs have all been socially important and beneficial in setting up defenses against the worst excesses of government and industry and arousing us to think in terms of alternatives to the traditional technological assumption. Anti-mobility, unfortunately, has become a by-product of some of these alternatives, primarily because of the obvious environmental degradation wrought by the automobile.[1] This means, then, that the cause of mobility has often been attacked on two fronts. It has been attacked by a variety of technological innovations and forces while it has been attacked, paradoxically, by those who have reacted, and sometimes overreacted, to the technological assumption.

In most instances the anti-mobility bias of those who question the technological assumption has not been thought out. One of the best thinkers of our times, E. F. Schumacher, has devoted some of his attention to it. He discusses mobility in the fifth chapter of *Small Is Beautiful*.[2] Before the advent of mass transport and mass communications, he points out, societies had a definite *structure,* an element that is vital to their development and permanence. Mobility and communication were in existence but *footlooseness* was not. Structure has now "collapsed, and a country is like a big cargo ship in which the load is in no way secured. It tilts, and the load slips over, and the ship founders."[3] The ultimate effect of all this needless movement is an unevenly dispersed population. The Southeast of England, for example, becomes overcrowded while other areas lack the advantages of development. The United States has a concentration of 80 percent of its people on 1 percent of the land. Third World countries see an unseemly and inordinate population crush in their urban centers. Later the "mobile, footloose society" (this time the terms are used together) sees a "law of disequilibrium" set in, for "nothing succeeds like success, and nothing stagnates like stagnation. The successful province drains the life out of the unsuccessful. . . ."[4]

Schumacher's mobility/footlooseness argument is framed within national borders, but it has implications for international travel and even for intra-community mobility. His concerns are natural and understandable, they point to an important problem, and they are rooted in altruism. There are, all the same, immense difficulties in this section of his work, for the basic problem is not so much a matter of defining mobility as of defining what he calls "footlooseness." He does not offer a precise definition, but since he contrasts the two terms at one point it can be assumed that he has no argument with exercise of the right of mobility. He recognizes its value and considers it neither illegitimate nor wasteful.

Footlooseness, however, can be deduced to be both wasteful and undesirable. It leads to tragic results. Development is hampered and is not sensibly grounded in any reasonable scheme of human settlement. The metropolis is an abyss of unemployment and a squandering of human, material, and spiritual resources. The hinterland is likewise depleted of these resources. The task of developing a society of humane, aesthetic, and permanent values is not merely made more difficult; it is undermined. It is therefore quite acceptable for one to undertake a journey or any lesser exercise of her or his right of mobility, but it is open to question whether the exercise of this right should be encouraged if it is going to lead to relatively permanent conditions of social, economic, and political churning and disruptiveness.

We have really resolved nothing at all, however, unless and until we can distinguish mobility from mere footlooseness, permanent moves from temporary ones, and the motives and desires of one human being from those of another. The feeling which comes through as one reads the fifth chapter and other essays and works of Schumacher is that he became disgusted, first, with the crass and insensitive features of everyday life in the West, typified by the automobile and our conspicuous lack of care for the land and the biosphere. He also became concerned with the same inane sets of assumptions about the world being foisted upon the Third World countries, especially in the form of useless, degrading, and neo-colonial aid and development programs. These observations of the West and of the Third World made him keenly alert to the dangers of profligacy and insensitivity fostered by the methods, patterns, and supposed purposes of much of the movement which goes on in the world. Footlooseness abounds, Schumacher wrote, and it causes considerable harm while performing no particular good.

Updating his work, it can now be shown that the settlement patterns and, more importantly, the values of the Western countries are changing. Appropriate technology, conservation of resources, communal and socialist values and settlements, and a strong rejection of crass, plastic materialism are receiving a hearing and are slowly changing the basic fabric of society. Population trends in the United States, in Canada, and to some extent in Britain point to dispersal. In the United States this has led to incidents in which those living in small towns demonstrated their resentment towards the in-migration of artists, crafts people, "hippies," farmers, and others who could very well be characterized as generally in accord with Schumacher's values of humaneness, beauty, and permanence. Politicians worry about changes in their constituencies, older people worry about having to contribute to school construction and costs and to social services,[5] and in some instances the governors of states, Oregon and Hawaii for example, have asked for no more new settlers. Despite such fears and conflicts, it can be concluded on a tentative basis that the most severe aspects of footlooseness seem to be working themselves out in the Western countries because of new and more dispersed patterns of settlement. Even the automobile is faced with finite space and increased fuel costs which must result in making it impractical on the scale of many more persons than in the past. In the Third World urbanization patterns and population growth show no sign of abating, but these problems constitute more than those of footlooseness. A host of economic, social, neo-colonial, and value agendas come into consideration which yield little hope of dealing with Third World problems from this kind of perspective.

Returning to how to draw a line between mobility and footlooseness, it appears that this is not really possible. One person's footlooseness is another's necessary exercise of the right of mobility. Individuals must judge their use of this right with the least possible interference from others. Mobility is not an absolute right, of course, for all sorts of considerations, including the rights of others, can reasonably inhibit or forbid it.[6] When its exercise seems reasonable or harmless, however, there must be a strong presumption in its favor. Footlooseness refers essentially to a lack of utility in movement, but utility cannot be sought in all things. It is necessary at times to exercise a right of movement for no particular given reason or for a reason that is no one else's business. It is sometimes even necessary for certain individuals to escape, to fade into anonymity or even into a different identity. No control of any reasonable exercise of the right of mobility is really necessary in the good society.

If what Schumacher called footlooseness persists to this day in American society, this may signify that the closing of the frontier, that important psychological as well as physical concept, has not quite occurred. But people seem to sense that the closing is not far away if it has not already occurred. Precisely when this limitation upon our movements and upon our aspirations and opportunities did take place is a subject for argument. It may have been when people stopped moving into Los Angeles County at the rate of one thousand per day, or it may have been at that important turning point in 1975 when migration from large cities to small towns and rural areas reversed the traditional pattern.[7] It may have been symbolically ushered in by Earth Day in 1970. One could pick 1973, a year of abrupt and earth-shaking changes, a year of cars lined up at filling stations to get some gas before the last drop ran out. Whenever it occurred, the realization of the closing of the frontier—of the using up and settlement of all the choice pieces of land in the country—changed the psychology of the nation and awakened it from a somnolence and apathy which had first set in back in the 1950s and remained largely undisturbed even in the 1960s.

The most recent and obvious example of this realization is the land and property craze, with plots of Midwest farmland going for uneconomic prices up to $5000 per acre and ordinary crackerbox houses in southern California fetching prices well in excess of $100,000. Long lines of couples wait for the sale of the last reasonably priced tracts of homes to open, and some developers have to resort to lotteries to see who gets into their houses and who will be kept out. These pressures, and the barely disguised fright and insecurity which fuel them, are at odds with the right of mobility, for once the latecomer who barely made it into the last project or the last house has settled in, he or she will be very careful about who else moves in or tries to move in, knowing that it is no longer easy to move again. This helps to explain why the politics and social outlook of environmental groups, neighborhood associations, and no-growth groups are neither always tolerant nor enlightened.

The powerful dynamics of the anti-mobility forces in present-day America are, in sum, grounded upon technological developments which hinder, inhibit, and threaten mobility. The reaction of groups— some altruistic, some selfish—against technology and growth, who see mobility as a kind of footlooseness or who see it as a threat, and an atmosphere in which an uneasy realization that the psychological as well as the physical frontier has closed—has made people wary, conscious of their "turf," and unsympathetic towards those who are less mobile, less well placed, and less fortunate.

This formulation demonstrates a further paradox of the mobility issue: that a large proportion, perhaps a majority, of the American public is aware of the issue when it is stated in a variety of forms— development, immigration, transportation, or urban-suburban relations, for example—but this same public seems only vaguely aware of any connection of these issues or of the linkages which can be established under the rubric of the right of mobility. A host of issues lend themselves to these linkages—busing in order to achieve school integration, the right of tenants to have and raise children in homes where the landlord has established an "adults only" rule,[8] the questions raised by institutions such as nursing homes—and deserve further study with a view towards effecting social and political change, but it appears that six issues have become most prominent in recent years and particularly lend themselves to a comparison of public policies and concerns on mobility. These are development, immigration, the physically limited, transportation, taxation, and issues related to governmental structure in the United States, including urban-suburban relations and federalism.

Development. The days of growth for the sake of growth are ending. There are, to be sure, instances of short-sighted planners and local authorities combining with developers to produce new strips and rectangles of ugliness across the countryside, but a new consensus seems to have developed which gives a low priority to growth and a much greater emphasis to preservation. There is also little likelihood that rapid, topsy-turvy development on the scale which occurred in post-war America in places such as Long Island, Tampa Bay, San Jose or Orange County, California, or the peripheries of most cities, will occur again in the near future. Water shortages, land scarcity, competing uses such as recreation or wildlife refuges, environmental considerations, and restrictions on the right of mobility all militate against it. There is, in addition, an aesthetic preference for keeping open spaces open as well as a growing awareness that much of the cost of development is borne by the taxpayers rather than by the developers.[9] Post-war suburban development did provide, of course, for mobility of a kind, since FHA and VA mortgages and vast outlays for highway construction created incentives for low-density, single-family dwellings to be built on what was then relatively cheap land. A similar trend has been brought into being by the Housing and Community Development Act of 1974, which encourages low-density construction and growth in unincorporated areas of urban counties.[10] These incentives have only created mobility of a kind, however, since they have proved to be vital in the formation of several versions of American apartheid—the separation of white from black, of the middle class from the poor, and of young married couples from other age and social groups. It also has created mobility of a meaningless and even energy-wasteful kind by requiring long commuting trips for the suburbanites, while at the same time public transportation has died on the vine.

All this is now well recognized, but this recognition has meant entrenchment of suburban attitudes and the development of a siege mentality. The Burger Court has accommodated these attitudes with decisions like *Arlington Heights, Warth v. Seldin,* and *Bradley v. Milliken.*[11] Suburban residents seem to demand social and racial homogeneity.[12] Again the closed frontier syndrome is at work as well as an aversion towards technology as represented by more automobiles, highways, apartment houses, and noise. A variety of devices have been set up to prevent or limit growth, in-migration, and development, including population "caps" and numerical limits in Boca Raton, Florida, and Petaluma, California, control of the number of construction permits in Ramapo, New York, control on types of construction through zoning laws in Arlington Heights, Illinois, and a moratorium on water meter installation in Santa Barbara and Goleta, California.[13]

Innovative approaches are called for, and some are being devised. One of the most important proposals in recent years is set out by Robert C. Ellickson in a prizewinning article in the *Yale Law Journal.*

Ellickson believes that the suburbs increasingly recognize economic and social advantages of no-growth ordinances, and that it will be difficult to prevent the adoption of such laws. Legislatures are loath to interfere with this, and property owners derive a large and tangible economic benefit through this control of the local real estate market. Tenants can be hurt by such laws because the increase in property values effected through this market manipulation will cause rents to rise; but tenants are usually not organized as well as property owners, according to Ellickson, even when they represent a majority of the city's population and voters. Ellickson therefore advocates the right of suburbs to establish growth controls, but also sets out the case for excluded persons to have a right to sue for money damages against the city if discriminatory practices can be shown.[14] This is presently not recognized in the law, but it is a proposal that should be commended for its innovativeness and for its recognition of the right of mobility. It nevertheless appears to be deficient for two reasons: (1) it sets up a presumption against mobility; the person seeking to exercise a right of mobility must initiate action rather than those who have established barriers against it; and (2) money damages are no remedy at all in a day of clogged courts and expensive and time-consuming legal services.

Solutions to the question of development are therefore difficult to devise, and make no mistake, development is no cure-all for the right of mobility nor, as the post–World War 2 experience amply demonstrates, does development necessarily enhance mobility. No-growth and controlled-growth partisans can also point out that no correlation exists between development and the creation of wealth in a locality. Fast-growing areas have often remained poor; likewise slow-growth areas have often retained their economic position.[15] A further complication for the right of mobility cause is that it has been criticized for being a tool of special and selfish interests such as developers and construction companies. This is nothing to worry about, for such a coincidence of interest is bound to arise in the kind of interest-group politics that is sometimes played in American local governments. It can also be shown that no-growth advocates and environmentalists are sometimes equally in league with the privileged and do a good job of protecting their interests.

A few guidelines are in order if development is to be sensibly based as well as protective and promotive of the right of mobility. The first rule should be, "Do not create enclaves." Diversity of peoples can lead to tolerance, and it has a further virtue of providing a potential barrier against exclusivity. It is rather difficult to argue in favor of keeping out a certain group if members of that group are sitting in the same room with the one who is to make such an argument. A lack of diversity in a local or neighborhood populace also makes for dullness. This is why the Swedish government houses the elderly in ordinary homes and apartments instead of singling them out for "retirement communities." Planners are beginning to recognize this and are moving away from setting up so-called homogenous housing projects and neighborhoods, and federal law is now moving strongly in the direction of protecting the physically limited so that they may mingle freely with non-limited people. There is no question that some groups and individuals may prefer to associate with certain groups and not with others, and there is no reason to believe that we could or even should outlaw preferences; but we must outlaw discrimination and exclusivity, for they are undemocratic, they breed prejudice, and they cannot be justified morally. Many suburbs, neighborhoods, retirement communities, and apartment projects have been conceived and built around such prejudice and are therefore outrageous people-classification systems with "unwelcome" mats in front of their doors. Legal and policy recognition of the right of mobility will break down these systems.

A second guideline is to recognize the need for small-scale development. This is incorporated into the purposes of the Housing and Community Development Act of 1974, the HUD Urban Homestead program, and other legislation, but the term "development" still tends to conjure up, in most of our minds, a large-scale project or commitment. Development (or redevelopment) can, however, be applied to a single dwelling or an apartment house. The application of effort on this scale also tends to promote diversity within local groups rather than enclaves. It will prove to be economical in terms of our resources—land, energy, and building materials—because small-scale development is undertaken by those who cannot afford to do otherwise and because it can help to reverse the great American tendency to destroy existing structures at a relatively early age and build new ones in their place. Small-scale development has a side benefit of promoting beauty as well, for it preserves the best of the past while avoiding the jarring duplication and sameness of large-scale development projects. Most importantly, small-scale development tends to obviate the leap-frog effects associated with large-scale projects, so that it fits more readily into the mobile but compact, high-density, energy-economic, public transport-oriented model of the city which seems best able to meet our future problems, circumstances, and imperatives. Small-scale development is therefore more likely to enhance the right of mobility.

A third guideline, which applies primarily to large-scale developers, is that the cost of development should be shifted from the taxpayers to the developers. This seems not only just but also economic in the sense that large-scale projects will be undertaken only under optimal circumstances. The cost, under this arrangement, will ultimately be borne by the owners and tenants situated in the development project, not by the taxpayers, who already suffer too many tax inequities and who have no particular interest in large-scale development or in extending the periphery of the city, as is often required, in order to accommodate it.[16] In many cities, particularly in the Snow Belt areas of the Northeast and Midwest, this is no longer an acute problem. The problem is rather the opposite but related one of attracting development, particularly industrial and other job-providing development, to replace that which has left for the sunnier climes of Georgia, Texas, and California. It is perhaps the most shameful aspect of mobility policy in America today that those fictitious persons we call corporations make great use of their right of mobility, sometimes to the detriment of real persons who are in no position to exercise their right of mobility, in order to shop around on a continuing basis for the best state and local tax deal, for the most primitive social welfare system, for the least unionization and worker militance, and for the most pleasant kind of climate, economic as well as meteorological, in which to do business. Development, taxation, and labor and social welfare policies of any locality must remain in a state of flux, often an agitated flux, as long as this auction-like atmosphere continues to exist.[17]

The last guideline is obvious but needs to be stated, and that is to bear in mind that there is always development, construction, and change going on in any locality, and that the most important question usually is, what kind of development? Different kinds of development will affect the right of mobility in different ways, and an assessment of this impact is absolutely necessary in the light of this country's post-war experience. How will a particular project help or hinder public transportation? How does it affect pedestrians? What effect will it have on land prices and on the environment? Who will bear the costs of development?

The right of mobility must be given an eminent place in such calculations even though it has been given short shrift in the past.

Immigration. Ample demonstration that the right of mobility is the right "we are not ready for"[18] is shown by the broad and deep concern aroused by the issue of illegal immigration in this country. Law enforcement agencies, a special group of congressmen, and the Immigration and Naturalization Service have been sounding the alarm, and a recent government report cites a welter of facts and statistics to support the claim that the problem is out of hand:

1. Illegal aliens in the United States are estimated to range up to 12 million, and only a quarter of these are employed.

2. A 1975 study shows that illegal aliens cost taxpayers in this country $13 billion or more per year in public assistance, medical, and educational expenditures.

3. The number of illegal Mexican aliens apprehended increased from 29,700 in 1960 to more than 680,000 in 1975.

4. INS simply does not have the problem under control as the torrent of illegal immigrants continues to flood the country, bringing drugs, crime, disease, and other illegal aliens with them. The Federal Advisory Committee on False Identification estimates that false identification crimes by illegal aliens amount to $3.6 billion per year.[19]

A variety of interest groups also feel that they have a stake in the issue. Labor unions, including Cesar Chavez's Agricultural Workers Organizing Committee, oppose illegal immigration because they feel that wage levels and the union cause are undermined by it. Some Chicano groups, as well as other ethnic associations, favor a more open and lenient policy. They believe that the INS has abandoned some of its traditional service functions in order to concentrate upon policing aliens. Racist groups are alarmed, as they always are, at the prospect of immigration leading to population growth within those sectors of the community of whom they disapprove. The Ku Klux Klan actually set up "border patrols" for a few days in southern California in 1977.

There is a general concern about the issue as well. A Gallup poll commissioned by the INS in 1976 showed that 74 percent of the people surveyed thought that illegal immigration is a serious problem.[20]

Illegal immigration is unquestionably a thorny issue, and more than that, it is an issue of great importance. Those who support the right of mobility must take an informed and understanding view of it, and this strongly implies recognition of the issue as one of hemispheric, if not world-wide, scope. The United States is not unique among Western, industrialized, rich countries of the world, for all these countries—Britain, West Germany, France, Scandinavia, the Low Countries, Canada—are faced with the issue of illegal immigration. Switzerland has been the scene of hot debates on exclusion of foreigners, and has even had a national referendum on the question, but all these countries, and most emphatically the United States, have experienced a "labor shortage" problem because their own citizens hold an utter disdain for the more menial jobs that are available and need to be done. The United States is unique in one important way: its border with Mexico is the longest and most direct point of contact on the globe between a developed country and a Third World nation. As long as this border exists and as long as the huge disparities in American and Mexican living standards remain, pressures for immigration, legal and illegal, will persist. This by definition limits the choices in any public policy resolution, or attempted resolution, of the issue.

An examination of the question of illegal immigration in the broadest context can therefore lead only to the conclusion that it is an understandable and inevitable phenomenon. Who can blame anyone for going to "El Norte" in order to broaden his or her opportunities to participate in the good life? Mexican and Latin American people hear from their friends and neighbors about their experiences, and in many cases they also receive the not-very-subtle message of American television and its idealization of the United States suburban lifestyle. Their response closely fits the behavior pattern eulogized in American mythology—the seeking out of a new land, individual initiative, the doing of something to rise above one's economic and circumstantial plight. In their case, however, they receive condemnation for acting out the American dream.

Some of the pressures and fears that are brought to bear against immigration are understandable, though certainly not those motivated by racism. Unemployment, crime, the lowering of wage standards, and pressures on education are certainly undesirable when these are known to exist. There is, all the same, undue alarm. The jobs taken are usually taken from no one, the illegal immigrants pay taxes, and many of them, despite their exposure to the American dream as expounded on television, return to Mexico. The figures on illegal immigration, whether they are those cited above or any others, are by definition inaccurate and suspect. The most acute problem associated with illegal immigration has in fact been the exploitation of the immigrants themselves by unscrupulous American employers. If any further legislation is really needed to deal with illegal immigration, this problem should be recognized and the onus of illegality should be put upon the employers rather than upon those whose only crime is that of seeking a job and a better life for themselves in the States. Once again, as with all mobility issues, there must eventually be a presumption in favor of movement, though in this case it has to be tempered by such exigencies as the status of the law and the need to weigh this presumption against legitimate national welfare objections. Some restrictions on immigration are inevitable and may even be necessary until that time when we can embrace, as a nation and perhaps as an international community, the unfettered right of movement of peoples across the face of the earth.

The worst effect of the immigration issue is what it is causing us to do to ourselves. Dangerous legislation has been introduced in Congress which could easily lead to the establishment of a national pass law. Casting a wide net over all of us in an attempt to solve the more narrow and specific problem of illegal immigration, a group of House members has proposed the issuance of a forgery-proof, laminated Social Security card to all those entitled to have one. Any potential employer must then refuse to hire anyone who fails to produce this card. The same legislation also provides for reestablishment of the bracero program of temporary employment of aliens which was abandoned in 1964.[21] Most of the sponsors of these proposals are Sun Belt legislators who are interested in improving access to cheap labor for the agri-businesses in their states; but at the same time, says one of the sponsors, Robert K. Dornan, Republican of California, "the United States is no longer a developing nation in need of huddled masses to conquer geographical frontiers."[22] (Again the "closing of the frontier" is in evidence as an anti-mobility factor.)

These House members demonstrate an amazing capacity for self-deception. In the first place, who has ever developed a forgery-proof card? How will illegal immigration be prevented when temporary workers will still be brought into the country? Much more important, these legislators are the types who are always alerting us to the dangers of Big Government. What could be bigger than this? B. F. Sisk, a California Democrat who also backs these proposals, assures us that there is a difference between these and a national identification card system.[23] What is this difference? It is difficult to find an area of our lives that is any more important than our employment. Later amendments to this legislation or, more likely, an administrative order from some efficiency-minded bureaucrat, could lead this country into a system of internal passports.

It is hard to overestimate this danger. Internal passports are invariably a characteristic of undemocratic systems. *Mobility control* is an important feature of South African life today, just as it is in Chile and the Soviet Union, and was in Nazi Germany. This is probably why the American public, in a Gallup poll reported in June, 1977, rejected the idea of a national identification card, though by an uncomfortably close margin of 50 percent to 45, with 5 percent undecided.[24] A Justice Department task force, the Federal Advisory Committee on False Identification, rejected the concept of a national ID card in June, 1976.[25] Secretary of Labor Ray Marshall, who also opposes a national identification card, supports the laminated Social Security card legislation of Sisk, Dornan, et al. He recently exposed his naiveté by saying, "If they can make a card that gives me money at the bank at night when nobody is there, and I can buy goods in the store with a card which only needs a phone call to check my card number, then I think we can make a noncounterfeitable social security card for workers to use when they are getting jobs."[26] Recent experience and revelations concerning the FBI, the CIA, Army Intelligence, and a host of other government agencies can hardly be reassuring.

The outlook, then, is not a cheerful one if this kind of legislation is passed. Those who know or learn how to forge identity cards will do so, as even Congressman Sisk admits.[27] The issue of illegal immigration will of course persist, but the American citizenry, who may have no involvement or concern with this issue, will face a totalitarian potential of invasion of privacy, harassment, and denial of mobility. Movement, as well as an anonymity which can sometimes mean freedom, could become impossible. It is doubtful whether the state needs to know so much about our lives or our movements.

The Physically Limited. The right of mobility is applicable to all persons, but its absence is most felt by those who are physically limited—

the "handicapped"—who, because of an accident, a birth defect, or a crippling disease, cannot move about as readily or as easily as the rest of us do. The plight of the physically limited and, not incidentally, the recognition that mobility in our society refers to both social and physical needs, brought about the passage of laws by Congress in 1973 and in 1975 which are aimed at relieving the problems faced by this important and heretofore neglected group. The central consideration and effect of this body of laws is that "no otherwise qualified handicapped individual . . . shall, solely by reason of his handicap, be excluded from the participation in, be denied the benefits of, or be subjected to discrimination under any program or activity receiving federal financial assistance."[28] The Rehabilitation Act of 1973, along with milestones such as the Education for All Handicapped Children Act of 1975, has served as a symbol of Congress's will and, it is to be hoped, by extrapolation, of the will of the people of America that we begin to recognize that equality of treatment, of opportunity, and of mobility must be accorded to the physically limited.[29]

Laws do not become operative, however, merely because Congress passes them. They require execution. In the case of the Rehabilitation Act, it appeared for four years to be nothing more than a sentiment of Congress, a matter which could have more appropriately been made the subject of a congressional resolution than a public law. Only in a very few places, such as the University of Illinois campus at Urbana, did the physically limited receive more than a nod in their direction, and this limited number of places existed before passage of the Rehabilitation Act.

Implementation finally came when executive orders were issued by Health, Education and Welfare Secretary Joseph Califano in April, 1977.[30] Califano's acquiescence was not easily won. It had been one thing for Congress to express humanitarian support for the physically limited and their mobility cause, but it was quite another to implement an expensive set of requirements which would cost $5 billion or more. The physically limited citizens of America had to escalate their tactics sharply, from simple letter writing and phone calls to sitting in at the HEW headquarters in Washington and demonstrating in front of Califano's house. The conduct of the HEW secretary throughout this period of protest seemed to change from day to day, passing through phases which were first conciliatory, then rejectionist, then dilatory, and finally cooperative.[31]

Califano's order has now filtered down to the state and local agencies, universities, schools, health centers, and public buildings which are the objects of federal assistance of one sort or another, and these are now proceeding to redesigning, rebuilding, removal of obstacles, construction of ramps, and other changes necessary for full implementation. A whole range of policies of federal grants-in-aid programs will be affected. Schools, for example, will probably need to reassess such matters as health care measures, counseling, and even athletic programs. Despite all this movement, definitive answers on some important questions are still to be found. One question, for example, is what policy is to be followed by public transportation companies. Are the physically limited to be given access to bus services provided for the general public, or are only special buses and equipment to be used for them? The public transportation industry claims that it can provide special services for the physically limited which will obviate the need to provide regular line service and that regular bus schedules cannot be maintained if the physically limited are to be accommodated. In Chicago this issue is now in the federal courts, with the plaintiff asserting a constitutional right to public transportation. This points out the possibility of a right of mobility amendment to the Constitution, wrought by judicial interpretation or perhaps even by the formal amendment process, but it also brings into focus the question of whether the right of mobility can be asserted against bureaucratic claims of efficiency of service and administration. Transit companies presently extend themselves to accommodate the elderly, parents with small children, even baby strollers, and on occasion the physically limited, so that a policy of inclusion of the physically limited into regular services may not prove to be so difficult as it is believed to be; in any event, this controversy again highlights the new awareness of the right of mobility and the need for its promotion and acceptance.

Implementation of the Rehabilitation Act of 1973 still requires some definitive answers, therefore, on the issue of access to public services and facilities. In addition, implementation of the legislation providing education for the physically limited will call for definition and refinement. The broadest possible leeway must be presumed for the physically limited if we are truly committed to equality as an ideal of American society. This moral imperative is complemented by a practical consideration: we cannot and must not continue to waste the valuable human resources represented by physically limited people. Society, to say nothing of the economy, needs these people and their ideas, talents, and contributions.

The next obvious goal for the cause of mobility of the physically limited is a broad and general application of the principles of the Rehabilitation Act of 1973, so that all sectors of society and of the economy dealing with the general public—even those defined as private—are required to end all discrimination and, insofar as it is possible, all social and physical constraints upon mobility. Whether a business firm, factory, hospital, hotel, restaurant, or office building receives federal assistance or not, it should provide equality of mobility, treatment, and opportunity, within the compass of its property, for the physically limited.

In the meantime the obstacles are great, the barriers are often insurmountable—and the curbs remain in place.

Transportation. The right of mobility appears to be most often suggested in discussions and treatises on the transportation issue, particularly urban transportation. In the past ten years the right of mobility concept has made its most obvious appearance in that genre of social and political writings which might be called the anti-automobile literature. The Ralph Nader study *Unsafe at Any Speed* is probably the first important work of this kind.[32] Nader's concerns barely touched the issue, however, and the right of mobility seems to be developed more strongly as a popular concern in later works by Helen Leavitt, whose chief concern is highway construction in urban areas, by John Jerome, who concentrates on what he considers the outmoded utility of the automobile itself, by William Plowden, who takes a historical approach, by Emma Rothschild, who depicts the backwardness of the auto industry in a technological as well as social sense, by Ronald Buel and Kenneth Schneider, who discuss the ecological havoc wrought by automobiles, and by K. H. Schaeffer and Elliott Sclar, who advocate a multi-modal approach in the hope that this will at least be a partial solution to the quest for the right of mobility.[33] All these writers allude to the right of mobility and all of them appear to characterize mobility, either implicitly or explicitly, as a right. This concern is nonetheless set alongside other ideas which are given equal and occasionally overshadowing importance—energy consumption and waste, policies and attitudes of the auto industry towards its employees, technical imperfections of the automobile, environmental effects, and, above all, aesthetic objections to the presence of automobiles in urban and even rural life. There are strong and compelling arguments against the automatic financing of roads, the replacement of homes, parks, and businesses by expressways, and the gross extremes of automobile design and of the three-car and four-car families who prop up the industry's tastelessness and vulgarity through their own tastelessness and vulgarity.

These anti-automobile books are a useful literature, for they have done a lot of healthy debunking of the automobile, of the industry, and of the complexity of interests which have brought this single mode of transportation to its dominant and disproportionate place in American society. They have torn away the myths of efficiency and technical competence of the auto industry, creating a defensiveness in both car owners and the car industry on the subject of automotive technology. They have created the impression, and it seems to be a correct one, that the "closing of the frontier" is at hand for the automobile if it has not yet occurred. (According to John Jerome, this closing frontier point was reached with the production of the Chevrolet Impala in 1970.) From the standpoint of social science and policy analysis, however, the yield from these works, as might be expected, is less than satisfying. They are thought-provoking popular works, competent in their own terms but limited in their precision and too broad-ranging in their critiques to develop a policy focus with any degree of exactitude. The right of mobility therefore becomes lost in the shuffle of their many concerns, arguments, and ideas. The limitations of anti-automobile literature and research should not imply, however, that this kind of work has reached the end of its road, to use an unfortunate metaphor, for there are many dimensions of automobile ownership and the dominance of this mode of transportation—class dimensions and psychological dimensions often having little to do with transportation per se—which call for further investigation and which have been given scant attention.[34] Some of these are as follows.

1. *The social respectability symbol.* Automobile ownership and use demonstrate respectability in American society. Use of public transportation may be respectable conduct in some places, such as New York, Chicago, or Great Britain, but not in others, such as Los Angeles or American small towns. Automobiles, on the other hand, are always

respectable. In addition, the use of an automobile implies that one does not need to sit next to "undesirable" types of people.[35]

2. *The symbol of strength.* A car and its owner and passengers are "strong," while pedestrians, bicyclists, and others are "weak." The latter are occasionally mocked, jeered at, or run down by the former. Missiles are occasionally hurled at them from cars. Courtesies may be observed in traffic situations, but they are often breached in a way which suggests a throwback to the days when poor peasants cleared the streets in a hurry to allow unfettered and swift passage of the king's horses.

3. *The private enterprise, individualistic symbol.* Cars are often said to offer privacy, time to collect one's thoughts, a useful period of time when its driver can be alone. Public transportation is not only public; it is a cooperative, group-oriented phenomenon. A *relatively* classless society is created on a bus or tram, one which can even be called a community, if only in a temporary sense.

4. *The contributor to economic growth.* This is a strictly utilitarian dimension of class and the automobile, depending upon a belief that the car owner contributes to the economy and its growth because of the initial purchase of the vehicle and also because of the further purchases—tires, repairs, parts, fuel, etc.—which are supportive of the consumer society. Appeals have been made to the public by the automobile industry, and even by government officials, in slack sales periods on these simplistic grounds. The non-owner, non-consumer, is on these terms less valuable to the economy and to society.

5. *The participant symbol.* Car owners have demonstrated their will to participate in the exercise of "choice," both in the broad sense of affirming by "vote" (here, a characterization of "purchase") the consumerist vision of democracy and in the narrow sense of choosing from the literally tens of thousands of make-model-style-color-interior fabric-accessories combinations. This exercise of "choice" is looked upon as both desirable and important. Non-owners, the aged, the physically limited, and others have "dropped out," and are non-participants who are of a distinctly different class.

Understanding the right of mobility and its relationship to the transportation issue can also be enhanced by deeper research into other psychological aspects of automobile ownership and use. Psychology journals and articles depict some of these considerations: the car as a symbol of opulence, as a lovemaking aid, as a mechanism or weapon of violence towards others or as an instrument of suicide, as a sex symbol, as an extension of one's personality, as an emblem of speed, modernity, and sophistication, as an emblem of freedom, independence, and rebellion, and as a substitute for bodily functions such as walking, talking, or thinking.[36] The anti-automobile literature developed to date takes no account of these important associations and relationships.[37]

A second source of the concept of the right of mobility in the transportation field is found in some of the technical and policy approaches developed by transportation planners and the public transportation industry. Unlike the popular anti-automobile literature, these sources of development have tended to be cautious and perhaps even timid in expounding such a principle. The conceptualization of the right of mobility is incomplete in anti-automobile literature because it is developed as a reaction to the overpowering emphasis accorded over the years to one dominant mode of transport. The conceptualization that has generally been applied by planners, technicians, and policy makers of the transportation industry appears to be incomplete because it emanates from a source which carries the inferiority complex developed through decades of a "sick" transit industry. This industry bears the stigma of failing to make a profit while no like stigma attaches to profitless private transportation. Its operations employ management-personnel practices and approaches that have been, in the main, developed for other industries but are then applied, willy-nilly, to public transportation. Few transit system managers are zealous advocates of the public transportation cause, to say nothing of a right of mobility. *Passenger Transport* and other industry publications are cautious public relations efforts, enamored as much with bus paint designs and new bus company logos as they are with substantive transit improvements and innovations. Cosmetic concerns such as these seldom touch the right of mobility, even though the transit industry could find common cause with transit-dependent elderly and other groups who would promote the idea.

The right of mobility, all the same, has fulfilled a role in the innovations developed in transportation planning in recent years. The "Right of Mobility" scheme developed by the British government in 1976 provides a system of payments to the physically limited to ensure their access to transportation services. One does not have to use the concept by name, of course, to show that it serves at least as part of the rationale for free bus services, as in Hamburg, Germany, Adelaide, Australia, and downtown Seattle; for reduced fares; for "dial-a-bus," as in the Watts area of Los Angeles; for the rural bus system and travel voucher experiments in West Virginia; for the development of the Bay Area Rapid Transit System; for the "pedestrianization" of city centers and shopping malls throughout the Western world; for the disincentives for automobile use that have recently been developed in Berkeley, California, and in Nottingham, England, and in connection with expressway policies, now abandoned but hopefully to return, setting up exclusive lanes for buses and multi-passenger cars in Virginia and California.[38]

However extant and interesting such innovations are, they do not add up to a great quest for, or even a clear conceptualization of, the right of mobility. They do, on the other hand, lend credence to its need and its existence. Taken together with a variety of technical studies and findings which are produced outside the confines of the transit industry, they point to what may be a far-off but ultimate acceptance of the right of mobility.[39] But the prospect is one of ambiguity and haphazardness. By themselves these sources—transportation planners and the transit industry—are not sufficient, any more than the anti-automobile writers are, for the development and promotion of the right of mobility. There must be a clearly conscious attempt to link this right with law and public policy in transportation as well as in the other issue areas affected by it. In the meantime there is a great deal that must be done if the automobile is to become the servant rather than the master of our transportation systems.

The automobile will be with us for a long time to come, and its use is understandable and hardly objectionable in some areas of the country—rural areas, small towns (though transit has a role to play in these), and low-density places like Montana, Wyoming, or northern Maine. It is understandable in these areas because it represents mobility. In large urban areas it represents immobility for non-owners and non-users who must be inconvenienced by it or, as is often the case, are ignored simply because it is assumed by policy makers that everyone has a car or the use of one. For the car owner it is an unreliable, expensive, energy-wasteful form of transportation particularly unsuited for the five-mile-per-hour crawl down the rush-hour expressway. High population density should always dictate public transportation as the dominant mode in urban areas.

This has long been recognized by planners, public officials, energy experts, writers, social critics, and social scientists, but the automobile remains dominant. The next few years will see the resolution of battles over emissions standards and fuel economy standards, the Highway Trust Fund, now due to expire late in 1979, gasoline taxes, and the size of federal, state, and local commitments to public transportation. These battles will not be easy, for the auto industry is now on the counter-attack and it has shown that it will use every weapon in its arsenal—lobbying, campaign contributions, public relations, stroking of the consumer, protectionism against imports, and even electronic eavesdropping of Ralph Nader's conversations—in order to maintain and expand its position.

It should be remembered that not even the 1973 Arab oil boycott managed to turn this country around on transportation policy. There were, nevertheless, some heady days in the early 1970s for the environmental cause, for the advocates of public transportation, and for those who believed in a variety of alternatives to the car. Ridership increases on buses and subways, the "busting" of the Highway Trust Fund so that some of it could be used for public transit, and a federal commitment of more than $11 billion for public transportation assistance over a five-year period, as well as increased concern at state and local levels of government, all gave encouragement to these causes as well as some serendipitous support, in substantive as well as lip service forms, to the right of mobility.

Some of the momentum has been lost because of President Carter's indifference to urban transportation concerns and to urban problems generally. Perhaps more important factors are the frontal attacks made by the auto industry upon its critics and, most disappointing of all, the concessions to industry arguments and the abandonment of the anti-automobile cause which have developed among those groups which could have been expected to carry on in their traditional roles as critics. Most important of any factor, however, is the strong and consistent support for the automobile that is generated by the general public; this has proved to be Detroit's manipulable advantage in any transportation policy debate. The industry's victories are clear enough: delays in the adoption of emission standards, palliative measures, if any, to be adopted on the question of gas guzzlers, abandonment of experiments with special lanes for buses and multi-passenger cars, a continued pressure for expressway and road construction, and a renewed insistence upon the specious objection that public transportation cannot be permitted to operate at a deficit.

The industry's frontal attacks have been going on for some time, and the industry's leaders have taken different tacks according to their perceived needs. General Motors and Ford executives, for example, have often cited the continued need for big cars, not only because they are most profitable for Detroit but because of the supposed needs of consumers. Sometimes these arguments become poignant, as when a GM executive pointed out that it would be unfair to the millions of owners of recreational vehicles if Detroit stopped producing cars capable of towing them.[40] John Riccardo of Chrysler Corporation has abandoned the traditional rugged individualism of the industry and has forthrightly insisted that automobile companies such as his should receive government subsidies. With this in mind, Chrysler extracted £100 million from the British government in 1976 upon pain of plant closures. In late 1978 it appears that the plants will be closed anyway after their sale to a French auto firm. Then there are the glowing reports, such as the figures released in October, 1977, by the National Automobile Dealers Association which allegedly show that car buyers pay more for their cars today as well as for their operation and maintenance, but after all, they are getting a better car than ever before for about the same percentage of their total incomes.[41] It is interesting to contrast this claim with Emma Rothschild's findings on the facade of modernity represented by the American auto industry's technology, with John Jerome's book on the engineering flaws and practices of Detroit, and with the statistics, now at new record levels, on recalls.[42] A Hertz Corporation study published in July, 1978, shows that the average cost per mile of owning and operating cars and trucks has risen since 1972 by 84 percent—nearly twice the nation's overall inflation rate of 45 percent during the period.[43]

Topping all the industry's propaganda is Barry Bruce-Briggs's apologia *The War against the Automobile*, which asks us seriously to accept that urban expressways are no great blight, that public transportation helps the well-off and the middle class at the expense of the poor (apparently they abandon their Cadillacs and Buicks for the bus), and that a new class of those awful people—journalists, academics, and bureaucrats—is seeking to choke off access by the masses to the cars they love.[44] Bruce-Briggs's theme is simple: America's system of auto-centered transportation is democratic, the best in the world, and the envy of other nations. All other transportation systems are "inferior,"[45] and the answer to our transportation problems is to "expand the auto-highway system and adapt the rest of the transportation network to it."[46] Cars give us speed, comfort, security, and the pleasure of driving, and, he adds, they also give us a handy weapon to use against others should the need arise. A great feature of car ownership, and others have noted this, is privacy, a place to think, to sing to ourselves, to dream our dreams. Supposedly we will watch the road and the traffic as we do this, and we may occasionally reflect upon the absurdity of building 113 million metal and plastic cubicles so that we can obtain privacy: this could be done more cheaply and efficiently without building cars.

Seeking to debunk the criticisms of the anti-automobile literature, Bruce-Briggs tortuously argues through the issues of air pollution, emissions standards, and the energy crisis. On emissions he points out that, after all, "nature itself does not provide clean air."[47] Noise? He suggests that you move away from the freeways and major thoroughfares if you do not like it. Does the auto stand for discrimination against the poor and racial minorities? No, this argument is "specious."[48] Destruction of the city? Well, urban living is "archaic," anyway,[49] and if the city dweller believes that life is difficult, consider the relative disadvantage of the suburban dweller, who has to fight his way downtown from a peripheral location through the rush-hour traffic. What about traffic control and enforcement and highway carnage? We would need crime control even if the auto did not exist. A motif of "this is how the game is played" and "this is how our wonderful capitalist system works" is dominant from start to finish.

This great democratic and efficient system has had a plot operating against it for some time, Bruce-Briggs says. Those limousine liberals of academia, the bureaucracy, and the press dislike democracy in transportation, it seems, and they want to get the working class off the road and into public transportation. A few seconds of thought or a resort to common sense will demonstrate that this plot is a house of cards. Academics, as everyone knows, work odd hours, teach night classes, keep to strange research schedules; they cannot care about the rush hour because they are not in it. Journalists invariably sleep until ten or maybe noon. That leaves only the bureaucrats, who do drive through rush hour traffic, but their craftiness should give us little worry if Bruce-Briggs's depiction of the Urban Mass Transit Administration, the Bay Area Rapid Transit System, and other agencies is only one-tenth accurate. These bureaucrats and agencies are either the most inept institutions ever created or they are totally subverted by automobile, oil, and highway interests. So much for the plot. Unfortunately, Bruce-Briggs cannot spot a real plot when he comes across one, for he dismisses the Snell Report, *American Ground Transport*, issued by Congress in 1974, as the work of an "incompetent" who hates General Motors.[50] Bruce-Briggs's only concession is that the anti-trust convictions and the conspiracies documented by Bradford Snell might "give some substance to the theory" that GM had a lot to do with the rigging of transportation systems in more than seventy cities.[51] How, he asks, were transit systems killed by substituting buses for trolleys? Snell tells us: by giving up an independent, fast, non-competing right of way.[52]

Ralph Nader, as one might expect, is a particular target in *The War against the Automobile*. General Motors President John Roche is taken to task for apologizing publicly to Nader for having him investigated, bugged, wiretapped, and harassed. Instead of apologizing, Bruce-Briggs suggests, the corporation should have issued this statement when it was found out (p. 130): "This fellow Nader was circulating a lot of lies about our products, so we naturally assumed that he was hired by one of our competitors. We still have not found out who he was working for, but we suspect Ford." If you assume from this that Bruce-Briggs's work has a certain graceless quality as well as an offensive moral tone, you are correct.[53]

Detroit's counter-attack leaves the morale of its critics intact, but other developments are more discouraging. *Environment* magazine, an old friend of the green movement, recently ran "The Auto Option," in which the case is set out for more energy-efficient cars, rather than public transportation, at a time when the oil-induced balance of payments deficit of the United States is approaching an annual rate of $27 billion.[54] Professor Alan Altshuler of MIT, returning to the campus after a stint as Massachusetts's Secretary of Transportation, has concluded in a forthcoming book that pressure on Detroit to produce more energy-efficient cars is the most feasible technical—and political—solution to our transportation and energy dilemmas. To his credit, Professor Altshuler recognizes the importance of the inequities fostered by auto-centered transportation systems, and therefore he seeks relief for the 17 percent of the population which has refrained, for financial or other reasons, from buying an automobile; but it is hoped that this distinguished researcher and urban expert can reexamine his conclusions on the future of the car in the light of its energy waste, the threat that it represents to urban space and to the quality of urban life, and the damage it wreaks upon the environment and upon the right of mobility.[55]

The willingness to live with more and more cars and with the social results they produce has always been evident to anyone who has left the meeting of an environmental group to go to the parking lot. Detroit knows, as we all know, that the automobile still rests upon a solid foundation of public support. Just look at a few surveys. Eight out of every ten Americans say that the car is their means of getting to work, and there is little to show that this figure will be modified in the near future.[56] A Gallup poll of October, 1977, shows that very few drivers would be willing to cut the number of miles they drive by as much as 25 percent in order to conserve fuel. The same poll shows that very few believe that it is necessary to do this.[57] The First Pennsylvania Corporation carried out a survey of executives recently, which was reported in the *Wall Street Journal,* and it shows that most of them would be willing to pay up to $2.08 a gallon before they would abandon the car as a means of getting to work. Another 20 percent said they would not give up their cars "at any price."[58]

It is clear that the Detroit counter-attack, and the acquiescence by some experts and environmentalists in some of the points made in this counter-attack or in a resigned feeling of the inevitability of the automobile, are buttressed by the public's devotion to the automobile society. A great deal of change must take place in the minds of the public if we are ever to come to grips with the imperatives of mobility, energy use, and the environment. Much of this mind set of course has been established by the narrow parameters of choice and of thought imposed upon us by elite decision-making processes. New ways of thinking about transportation alternatives and new processes of social and economic value orientation are possible, however, and this can be demonstrated by looking at other Western and industrialized countries and their public policies. Denmark is a good case in point; it now has a purchase tax on automobiles which is more than equal to the price of the car.[59] Canada, the country most comparable to the United States in terms of open spaces and urban design, has set up a stiff new gasoline tax.[60] Most European countries have higher gasoline taxes, license fees, and even ecology taxes. All of them have a much greater commitment to public transportation.

None of the foregoing should be interpreted to mean that the American public is not manipulated or that its choices are made within a national environment that is free of conspiracy and elite-dominated decision making. The facts and the record clearly counter any such assumption.[61] Leadership is needed, all the same, on the transportation issue from the White House, from politicians, from planners, social scientists, and other analysts, and most of all from the social conscience interest groups. The alternatives to the car are well known, and the specifics of a new transportation policy direction can and must be worked out with these alternatives in mind. Change will come sooner or later, but it will be less abrupt, less manipulated by the auto industry and the interest groups which support it, and easier to live with if it comes sooner.

Taxation. The transportation issue suggests, at several points, that a variety of tax reforms can be applied which will aid us in the transition to a society in which the right of mobility is recognized and encouraged, but tax measures can also effect changes in other areas of concern to the right of mobility and its supporters, and these certainly would include development, housing, immigration, and the rights of the physically limited and the elderly.

Long ago it was recognized that taxation can be used to achieve a variety of legitimate social objectives which go well beyond mere revenue raising. The most prosaic examples of this are probably the heavier taxes levied on tobacco and liquor than upon ordinary consumer items. The federal income tax itself came into being because of the recognized need to redistribute income and to regulate certain practices of business, industry, and society. As a general rule, it can be said that tax measures which are in accord with the goal of redistribution will tend to promote and enhance the right of mobility. Programs which aid the poor, the elderly, and the physically limited, for example, are presumed to be helpful in promoting social, and sometimes physical, mobility if these are paid for by those of us who are well-off or better-off than the beneficiaries of the programs. Like all broad principles this one is not invariable, and for that matter it is an intensely complicated business to determine who subsidizes whom as a result of any particular tax or budget measure. A perusal of the listings of the studies done by centers such as the Urban Institute, the Brookings Institution, the Joint Center for Political Studies, the MIT-Harvard Joint Center for Urban Studies, or the Ralph Nader Study Group will clearly reveal the question of subsidies to be a major preoccupation, whether these are subsidies between income groups, racial classifications, regions, urbanites and suburbanites, cities and unincorporated areas of metropolitan regions, bus riders and car owners, or whatever. A variety of conclusions are reached on a broad spectrum of tax and budget issues, but in general the principle as stated remains along with its corollary: that tax measures and budget decisions which subsidize the affluent, such as capital gains allowances, depreciation write-offs on apartment houses, or stock option shelters, tend to move our society towards greater social and physical immobility.

These are indirect effects wrought by general taxation and fiscal measures. More direct effects upon mobility can be traced to laws and rulings which help to define the present plight of our cities, our transportation systems, our social welfare systems, and our migration patterns by creating various incentives and disincentives for mobility. The tax credit for interest paid on mortgages, for example, has undoubtedly had some effect in promoting the low-density, car-oriented urban growth patterns that have emerged since World War 2.[62] Rentiers living in apartment houses in central cities are given one more reason, perhaps the decisive one, for abandoning a lifestyle in which urban values are cherished, public transit is important, energy is conserved, and mobility is maximized. The relatively low gasoline taxes which continue to persist in the face of an energy crisis and what seems to be a lethargic Congress are still promoting reliance upon the automobile as the center of our transportation systems.

All these assertions are testable, so that it is possible to derive conclusions about the alleged effects of a given taxation or budget policy. Once this technical question is answered, however, it is then possible to set tax and budget policy according to the values we wish to see governmental and social institutions reflect. Tax and budget questions ultimately become questions which help to define the kind of society we are to live in rather than questions of a technical nature, as some people seem to believe and as others would have us believe; and ideally one of the values we cherish is the right of mobility, which can be nurtured and aided by enlightened tax policy.

A general revulsion towards all taxation seemed to be shaping up in 1978. Congress was inundated with proposals and votes calling for deep tax cuts. The key to this attitude was found in the passage of various tax-cutting propositions by the voters in state referenda, including the overwhelming passage of Proposition 13 in California, a property tax-cutting measure. It is still too early to assess the effects of this tax-cutting mania, but a large number of urban experts, budget specialists, and even politicians are warning that this is a foolhardy course. Capital projects have been severely cut back and even maintenance of routine city services is threatened in the states which have passed these propositions. "California will have a due bill on urban maintenance in the 1990s that will knock your hat off," according to Fred Jordan of the National League of Cities.[63]

Tax cuts almost always are bad news for the right of mobility. The programs and services needed to implement the right of mobility will never see the light of day if they must compete with already established but badly pinched services and needs. An anti-mobility bias is also built into some of the tax-slashing measures. Proposition 13, for example, calls for a higher percentage of assessed valuation for a new owner of a home, which tends to make people stay put in their old home.[64] One must hope that the tax-cutting binge will not last long. Neither the country nor the right of mobility can afford it.

Governmental Structure. The structure of government appears to affect some of the problems associated with the inhibition and curtailment of the right of mobility. Specifically, those structural characteristics of the American system which seem to cause the most difficulty for the exercise of this freedom are (1) the artificial barriers created within metropolitan areas by municipal, and sometimes by state, boundaries; and (2) federalism, that division of the nation into fifty sovereign entities which is often praised, and just as often decried, for the effects it has on public policy in the United States.[65] In many respects these problems posed for the right of mobility by governmental structure are the most insurmountable of any, since they involve a panoply of traditions, the loyalties that are based in sectional, regional, city, district, state, and neighborhood differences, the vested interests of politicians and bureaucrats, a stake in the present scheme of things enjoyed by interest groups, and inertia.

The idea of suburbia is a much older one than many Americans realize. We tend to think of it as a post-World War 2 phenomenon; but in Britain, for example, it can be traced to the tenth century, when the area south of the Thames was first settled. Much further back in the past, according to archeological findings, a "Greater Ur" was built at distances up to three miles from the city.[66] It should also be noted that the history of the suburban idea is not without its happy accidents. Tel Aviv, for example, was founded early in this century as a suburb of Jaffa, but has grown to become one of the Middle East's most vibrant, exciting cities. In the developing countries, however, suburbia is often synonymous with poverty and squalor, for the great urban centers are often ringed with shantytowns filled with millions of hinterland peoples looking for a better life.

In America suburbia came into being shortly after the rise of our industrial and commercial centers in the last century. Suburban towns had experienced considerable growth by the time George M. Cohan's ditty "Forty-Five Minutes from Broadway" became a hit. Public transportation, whose advocates today bemoan the low-density patterns of suburban housing because they complicate transport planning, actually aided in early suburban development. Today more people live in the suburbs than in the central cities, and this development has brought immense problems with it, not only for the right of mobility or for transportation, but in housing, land use and zoning, schools, race relations, air and water quality, and public services. This has brought with it a deep sense of social malaise. The rise of suburbs has also brought in its wake a people-classification system which subtly imposes itself even upon those who might otherwise be city-inclined. Our system of social and economic apartheid cuts both ways, keeping certain social classifications out of the cities and others out of the suburban enclaves. The trite observation is often made that there are various kinds of suburbs—working class Hoboken, New Jersey, black Compton, California, and wealthy Kenilworth, Illinois; despite this variation in suburban models there is clearly a common point of reference implied by the term "suburbia"—and this is sometimes designated as the "sociological model"—which means predominantly white, predominantly middle class or wealthy, and given to a tendency to consider itself exclusive or semi-exclusive.[67] Suburban residents are sometimes known to compare their cities to exclusive clubs and to treat them and regard them as such.[68]

It is time to confront the truth that suburbia, despite its historic persistence as a human settlements phenomenon, is not an idea that is well suited to present-day needs. The problems of the city which the suburbanite seeks to escape—crime, inferior schools, bad housing, pollution—eventually catch up with the peripheral areas of the metropolis. The central cities subsidize suburbs by providing a disproportionate share of services and welfare costs within the metropolis. It is true that some studies claim that no great difference exists in costs and benefits accorded by cities to the suburbs and by the suburbs to the cities, but no study accounts for the myriad indirect costs.[69] Low-density suburbs are energy-inefficient, for example, in both transportation and housing, and this factor strains transportation and environmental costs.

Much more significant is the sense of apartness created by the artificial distinction of city and suburb, a distinction which ignores the reality that city dweller and suburbanite both are a part of, and their respective fates are bound up with, the city and the metropolis of which it is the center. In the discussion on development it was shown that recent decisions of the Burger Court have, unfortunately, encouraged this artificiality and apartness, but Arlington Heights is no less a part of Chicago than the Loop, and Livonia is no less a part of Detroit than Cadillac Square. Suburbs will exist in their present form for a long time into the future, but the sooner we recognize that we must do away with artificial barriers and enclaves and with the idea that some, but not all, of us are entitled to escape from problems while others must be left to deal with them, which is central to the present-day suburban idea, the better chance we will have of getting at the root of mobility problems and, for that matter, all urban problems.[70] In Texas, which seldom seems to serve as inspiration for the solution of social problems, the central city has annexation powers which prevent, or at least can prevent, the development of a multitude of suburban entities. Metropolitan integration through annexation, though it will be bitterly fought, must be a starting point towards urban solutions.

A push in this direction comes from a variety of federal agencies in the transportation, housing, development, and environmental fields, but often as not the regional arrangements set up tend to exacerbate urban-suburban differences and, on many occasions, to establish decision-making bodies in which suburban and rural interests are overrepresented. A variety of palliatives have also been proposed to meet the sharpening and tension-laden crisis which seems to be developing in urban-suburban relations: special districts which cross municipal boundaries, a right to sue for damages when a community has excluded individuals through adoption of no-growth statutes,[71] and some tax-equalization measures. Such proposals underscore the importance of the need for recognition of the right of mobility, but they do not come to grips with the problems of apartness and social exclusivity. Until metropolitan integration takes place and the idea of exclusivity is dispensed with, the burden imposed upon the right of mobility by urban-suburban differences in governmental structure will remain.

Federalism can also distort, and occasionally impinge upon, physical and social mobility. A number of constitutional provisions, such as the interstate commerce clause and the equal protection clause of the Fourteenth Amendment, have performed a service for the right of mobility and have caused the courts to protect this right through indirect means, but law and public policy in America have never developed to a point at which the right of mobility is directly protected. The fifty sovereign entities we call "states" have demonstrated time and again that they are willing to thwart the right of mobility in the name of some designated higher "good"—racial segregation, immobility of workers wrought through sharecropping arrangements and exploitation, for example, even by force, as in the Kentucky coalfields in the past, or simply by keeping "undesirable" people out of a state when they intend to migrate, as in California in the 1930s.

Contrast this with the simplicity and directness with which corporate mobility is expedited within America. Though corporations have no natural rights in natural law theory, as human beings do, they can move about, take good advantage of a variety of local conditions ranging from climate and resources availability to tax concessions and anti-unionism, and enhance their upward mobility in ways which are completely impossible for most people. They need not be incorporated within a particular state—they can be chartered in Delaware, that old corporate favorite, or some other place—in order to wreak havoc upon its environment, disrupt its social and economic life, distort its tax structure, break its labor unions, and use its resources. They pack up and leave at an opportune time which is invariably inopportune for the employees and other individuals who have counted upon it for their economic survival. These practices can have a variety of socially undesirable effects upon individuals' right of mobility, including the social and economic immobility imposed by unemployment and the inability to follow a corporate employer to its new location. Many companies give employment preferences to local residents in their new locations.

This set of difficulties is not easy to deal with, but a variety of solutions suggest themselves, including the federal registration of corporations, preferential employment rights for those who lose their jobs because of corporate moves, reforms in collective bargaining legislation such as those proposed in the 95th Congress, and a minimum federal tax on corporations which would be returnable to any state in which they happen to locate themselves.

It is quite useless, of course, for the advocates of social change to rail against federalism as a system. It was established by men who knew what they were doing, privileged men who realized that a separation of powers at the federal level combined with the areal division of powers into designated national, state, and local jurisdictions would be obstacles for the emergence of "faction"—interests organized to obtain legal as well as popular consent for their policy goals. In view of these constraints, it is better to look at federalism in the light of the opportunities it presents. Successful implementation of a new and socially progressive policy within the social and political laboratory of a single state can serve as a pilot for change. It is a rare phenomenon, but it can occur.

The right of mobility for individuals living in a federal system can be made effective only by striking down most state-imposed barriers and residence requirements which interfere with it, whether these be in the areas of voting rights, attendance at a state university, the right to take up residence, welfare rights, employment, or migration for any legitimate purpose. At the present time this is a hit-or-miss situation imposed by the particular features of legislation and case law and their interpretations, and it is only in the past half-dozen years that any significant attention has been given to the development of a right of mobility rubric for these matters in their relationship to federalism.

5

DECISION MAKING AND
MOBILITY POLICY

Political scientists and policy makers recognize the importance and centrality of decision making in the political process. The right of mobility and its attendant concerns are subjected to political decision making on an almost daily basis in a multitude of American governmental jurisdictions, and it is necessary to understand and assess the impact of this. It has been shown that the right of mobility is threatened and endangered by many of the trends in current policy making, and understanding why this is so depends in part upon an acquaintance with the decisions—and sometimes the non-decisions—which have brought about this state of affairs.

Not all the relevant data are available for a comprehensive undertaking which would lead to a full understanding of mobility decision making; and unfortunately, this is even the case when a single area of the mobility issue—development, for example, or immigration, or transportation—is analyzed. A better understanding of decision making may be possible if the analytical focus is narrowed to one of these areas; somewhat arbitrarily, transportation has been chosen for a greater in-depth look at decision making and its effects upon mobility. The extremely localized character of many development decisions and the fact that they are often hidden from public view militate against development as a choice. Immigration, by contrast, is totally national as an issue as far as decision making is concerned. Transportation, therefore, appears to be the likely issue to yield the greatest appreciation of decision making and its impact.

A further difficulty presents itself and cannot be easily resolved. There is a great divergence within social science on the question of an appropriate descriptive decision-making model for American politics, and there is ample reason for doubting that much progress has been made in community power studies since the days of the first debates between pluralists and elite theorists. Theories of synthesis have been developed, studies have been replicated using both the essential frameworks, aggregate data have been developed through coding and classification of the plethora of case studies, and the pluralists and anti-pluralists have both elaborated their critiques.[1] All of this effort has nonetheless produced cynicism and even despair among political scientists and sociologists, and though we may know more than we ever have about community power and decision-making models, some astute observers have hinted broadly that our knowledge may in fact have decreased.[2]

Decision making in transportation may appear, to the casual observer, as a highly diffuse set of arenas and actors. There is Congress, authorizing transportation legislation and the expenditures to support it; the executive branch, through a variety of agencies, enforces a myriad of regulations through the Department of Transportation, the Urban Mass Transit Administration, the Federal Highway Administration, the ICC, the aviation agencies, the maritime agencies, the Defense Department, and other offices and bureaus which may have more marginal, but still important, decision-making powers; then there are the states, the courts, the cities, the local transportation boards and agencies, regional administrations, bi-state compact administrations, and counties. Each branch, level, and agency of government is in turn affected by various interest groups, citizen groups, lobbyists, and "client" groups who demand a voice in transportation policy making. Many of the demands may conflict with one another, with some groups winning their demands on some occasions while others win at other times. This is a democratic system in action, or so it would seem.

We know better. Most transportation decisions made in government are, naturally, limited in their scope and effects. A bicycle path is to be built. A bus line is to be changed or improved. A road is to be widened. Members of transportation boards, county boards, city councils, and even state legislatures find that the parameters of policy making within which they are permitted to work can be narrow and restrictive, and the important guidelines for policy are invariably set up at the national level. But it goes further than that, for elite-group perspectives obtain a dominant position in most national transportation decision making.[3] An automobile-highway complex has held this dominant position throughout the post-war period in America, and some new emphasis on alternatives to the automobile has not altered this power configuration:

Our current policy emphasis is on still further development of the automotive-highway transportation system, an emphasis that is supported by a very large-scale commitment of the nation's resources. Mass transit is going nowhere, a fact that is assured by the automobile interests and their allies through their skillful use of an interlocking web of economic and political interests that extends across the length and breadth of the national economy. This great aggregation of power has been used to control our urban transportation policy and, in turn, to exert a powerful and detrimental impact on the quality of urban life.[4]

Even those observers who believe that changing patterns in transportation policy have now become important, such as Alan A. Altshuler, detect a certain sense of malaise. After pointing out that transit aid is one of the most rapidly growing of all federal programs over the past six years (yes, it is when it is compared to nothing), he reflects some of the mood in the transit industry by stating that "... indeed, even the operating subsidy claims made on behalf of new systems in recent years generally seem intended more to establish a tone, to communicate a hope and a recognition of taxpayer concerns, than to convey firm guarantees."[5] In the meantime public transportation often receives bad press notices even when these do not seem justified, and a powerful socialization process is imposed on the public by the press, by the education system, and by auto industry propaganda to convince it that the car is vital to our economic system and our way of life.[6] This is done to such an extent that the satirist Russell Baker has come up with a "solution" in which the government will "buy Detroit's annual production and dump it into the oceans on delivery. Thus we preserve the automobile industry, keep the economy booming and escape economic and ecological disaster."[7]

All this tends to point to C. Wright Mills's "power elite" approach, or the anti-pluralist approach, if you will, in analysis of the transportation issue. Mills's chief work, *The Power Elite*, was aimed at the military-industrial complex, but it ranged far enough to suggest that issues other than military spending were strongly directed by elite-power perspectives.[8] There are a number of important and helpful strengths in what may be called a Millsian or power elite approach.

First, this approach recognizes and emphasizes the integrated structure of institutions. It recognizes that the vast majority of, if not all, political actors seek to achieve results for one kind or another of institution, group, or interest.[9] (We are not, for the moment, considering such intangibles as ego satisfaction, personal monetary incentives, or the eagerness of an organizational staff to "do a good job.") Political issues and problems, at least the ones which count most, are usually defined in collective terms, i.e., by how a decision, non-decision, or compromise will affect the poor, the farmers, the AFL-CIO, the textile manufacturers, or the Navy. Two kinds of major activity in the American political process are, to be sure, defined in individual rather than in collective terms: individual political favors and court decisions. In the latter it is occasionally and perhaps justifiably asserted that they affect only the plaintiffs and defendants involved, but class actions and effects of precedent vitiate much of this argument. In any event, court decisions and individual favors are seldom considered important by pluralists, elitists, or any other students of power unless they have effects which are traceable to a broadly collective impact. It is not so important to know that General Jones went from a high defense post to the board of XYZ Corporation and later back into government service as it is to know that generals and admirals and business executives fit into this pattern of career behavior and that this pattern characterizes the behavior of the organizations concerned.[10] It is not so interesting, in and of itself, to know that links have existed between a number of secretaries of transportation and the oil industry as it is to know that government officials make decisions favorable to industry in return for what Ralph Nader calls "deferred bribes" and that a kind of musical chairs game pervades the relationship of government and big business.[11] It is also not very interesting or helpful to know, though pluralist works tell us this, that a variety of actors participate in local decisions in New Haven and other cities, decisions which are only of local concern and which are but remotely tied to national issues and concerns of any moment.[12] The Millsian power elite approach carries no such defects or illusions with it. It recognizes that the important integrated structures of national power are likely, indeed invariably, to be found in those areas of concern, like mobility policy and transportation policy, which can be assumed to be of great interest to the small elite which makes the most important decisions in this country, decisions which are of concern to the automobile-highway complex or the military-industrial complex, decisions involving government and corporate finance, decisions on farm and labor policy, and decisions on the establishment of national priorities. C. Wright Mills recognized that these power configurations are not only well integrated but that they produce decisions within a closed structure of exceedingly narrow policy choices, a system of "organized irresponsibility,"[13] and, though he was less explicit on this point, he intimates that the national power elite is integrated along both functional and areal lines.[14] This areal integration, so obvious in the case of the automobile-highway complex, is peculiarly important to our analytical purposes and is easily distinguished from a matter such as education policy in New Haven or some other city. Mills never believed that city boundaries or metropolitan or state boundaries represented the limits of power structures, national or local; and though this should be an obvious point, a number of pluralist writers have mistakenly said precisely this.[15] Mills recognized, in sum, that there is an important set of relationships developed between national and local elites despite the overwhelming importance of the former. (This is admittedly one of the weaker sections of *The Power Elite* and is not the major concern of the thesis he developed.)

Second, this approach provides a much needed and steady focus upon the narrow range of policy choices usually made available by elite forces in any given policy area. It can be further assumed that the maintenance of such a focus will help to explain the narrowness of range. Douglas Fox, in an excellent review of community power studies, says that we should become more concerned with "private" decision making which involves the establishment of priorities or the distribution of political resources. Further, ". . . very few community power studies have dealt with such private decision-making. To continue on this course is to say that capitalism is an irrelevant factor in the study of American power relationships, and that businessmen are unable to allocate resources."[16] The steady and necessary focus of the Millsian approach is obviously suited to this kind of investigation since it has always been preoccupied with such phenomena. The power elite must be as great a concern for the policy analyst as it is for the institutional analyst. Two major contributions have already been made to community power studies by policy analysts who clearly work within the Millsian framework. The first of these is a critique of the assumptions of policy analysis set out by Kenneth Dolbeare. The broad scale of concerns analyzed by Dolbeare go well beyond the scope of this study, but his article is well worth reading just for his remarks on some of the trends which have pervaded policy analysis over the past decade and for his realistic treatment of the often conservative term "realism."[17] The second is the famous Peter Bachrach-Morton Baratz contribution "The Two Faces of Power," which demonstrates with devastating effect that the pluralist emphasis on community decision making overlooks the decisions which are not made and which will never be made because the groups which would seek such goals have no influence. Bachrach and Baratz touch the heart of the right of mobility issue. They have been faulted for failing to set out a "rigorous" means of testing the frequency and substance of non-decisions, but it is readily conceded by almost all observers that non-decisions are a fact of political life at the community as well as other levels, our inability sufficiently to identify and analyze them notwithstanding. These critics are making a Gilbert and Sullivan demand, since non-decisions are by definition not capably analyzed.[18] Correlative to these contributions, though it does not fit perfectly into what might be called a Millsian tradition, is the important and innovative work of Murray Edelman on political symbolism.[19] The dimensions and perspectives of his work complement the contributions of power elite theorists by showing that manipulative politics, the kind of politics often fostered and promoted by elites, can be strengthened and enhanced by substituting symbolic change for substantive policy change. The contributions of Edelman, Bachrach and Baratz, and Dolbeare are meaningful for their own sake, but they are also helpful building blocks in the development of a Millsian approach to policy analysis and to the issue of transportation.

The third strength of the power elite thesis in understanding decision making is that it is devoid of any systems-maintenance bias. This is beneficial from both political and analytical dimensions—from the political because there is less fear of change and more of a tendency to produce change, and from the analytical because there is no fear of consulting some normative premises to ascertain whether some forms of power and its exercise are illegitimate. Systems-maintenance bias is a complaint which has become very familiar to pluralists, but it is no less pointed and serious for its familiarity.[20] In the long and boring debates which have been carried out with "value-free" social scientists and military analysts, among others, it is their prominent and ever-present Achilles' heel. To be devoid of systems-maintenance bias, to be sure, may even be considered a virtue, but like many virtues this one is linked with necessity in the form of a condition precedent for worthwhile social and political analysis; for analysis, whether it be concerned with institutions, policy, psychological dimensions, or whatever, must refer at some point to the needs of people and must seek to meet these needs.[21] Among the various defenses of systems-maintenance bias, obscurantism is the most effective, for it deflects critics and sometimes bewilders them. No direct defense of this bias is nearly so effective. Assumptions are quite plainly stated or implied in a direct defense; obscurantist statements and methods require deciphering and interpretation—at the very least, one will be told this—before the value-laden assumptions behind them can be criticized or analyzed. (There are, to be sure, some social scientists who describe the American system in broad terms as one of elite rule, but who also assert that it is good that the great and unwashed masses have relatively little to say about the decisions that are made.[22]) Obscurantism has therefore served the automobile-highway complex, the military-industrial complex, and other established interests well.

The concerns with systems-maintenance bias, obscurantism, and meeting the needs of people are closely tied to the fourth strength of the Millsian tradition: it defines institutions, policy, issues, and decision making in class terms. Admittedly, this has been an imprecise exercise at times. Mills, for example, defines Congress as being only in the middle range of the levels of power exercised in this country; this obviously leaves a great deal to be desired in terms of definiteness.[23] The term "class" itself is imprecise because of its various uses and overuses in social science, particularly sociological, literature. Mills is of course a Marxist and this helps to point the way in appreciating the implications of *The Power Elite* and his other works. For better or worse, it means that he tends strongly to direct his attention to the top of the pyramid of economic, social, and political structures. His works demonstrate that he was most concerned with the undemocratic and illegitimate accretion of power and perquisites which had become characteristic of the military-industrial complex. He performed his task so well that he awakened many Americans to this uniquely organized and unprecedented danger, including perhaps even Dwight D. Eisenhower; for too many others in government, the press, the social sciences, the professions, and the working class, these insights were not achieved until years after our involvement in Vietnam.[24] Mills's concerns did not call for a precise elucidation of class structure. Only a bare bones sketch was necessary and any further effort along these lines would have sidetracked him. The task remains undone, and important as it is, it should not be allowed to sidetrack anyone who wishes to focus upon a powerful elite complex and its ramifications. What is necessary is an awareness of the class dimensions of policy making. Few issues can be well defined without this set of dimensions, despite experimentation with "arenas of power" and other synthetic and pluralist models.[25]

The fifth and final strength of this approach is found in the attention given to mass socialization processes which make the maintenance of elite privilege and dominance possible.[26] These processes include the activities of the media, which were so important in shaping the Cold War in the American mind and establishing the groundwork for the dominance of the military-industrial complex, the parceling out of defense contracts, military installations, and other Cold War-inspired largesse so that a broad and dependent base of support for the war machine came into acquiescent existence, and other complementary processes—witch hunting and red baiting, for example—which facilitated the rise and the perpetuation of the complex. Analogous processes have been characteristic of the automobile-highway complex and other outrageously irresponsible centers of power.

These five basic strengths establish the adequacy, indeed the great advantages, of the Millsian approach as a basis for the study of community power, whether community is defined in local or national terms. It has already been pointed out that the power elite thesis is not complete, although some vital and even exceptional contributions have been added to it over the years. The interaction of national and local elites will require extensive elaboration. The dimension of federalism needs more careful investigation. Certainly the state level has been largely ignored by elite theorists; until now this has been left to policy institutes, many of which have been co-opted through close contacts with state government and the state central committees of the major parties, and with internship and public administration programs; or it has been left to policy analysts who correlate socio-economic characteristics of the states with institutional arrangements, who examine budgetary processes and results, who contradict the findings of one another, and do other things which are equally uninteresting.[27] The fact that these studies are not very interesting is the best that can be said about them; at their worst, they have chauvinistically glorified state government with an emphasis as misplaced as Edward C. Banfield's acceptance of the plight of the cities.[28] The relationship of local and national studies will require extensive work. Some of the conclusions drawn up so far are quite dubious, such as G. William Domhoff's assertion that Robert A. Dahl's New Haven study and C. Wright Mills's *The Power Elite* are compatible.[29] The narrow focus of the Dahl study of decision making and his failure to place local decisions in a broader context are enough to show that a basic incompatibility exists. Elite theory needs to move into more issue areas. The military-industrial complex must receive continuing attention, but it is past time that other issues and concerns should be examined; foremost among these is the issue of the automobile-highway complex, for the skewed priorities created by it represent an intrusion into a whole range of human concerns, not the least of which is the right of mobility.

The strength of the Millsian approach may still not be obvious to pluralist critics after it has been set out; but it is also interesting to note that it may not be obvious to some Marxists either. Mills's credentials as a Marxist have been called into question because he asserts that "power elite" is a much more descriptive and workable term than "ruling class." He prefers to leave open the question of whether a ruling class rules through the power elite, but he makes it clear that the class dimension is very important. He allows for co-optation and a limited recruitment of individuals into elite positions, and more importantly, he looks upon the power elite as a ring of "establishments" rather than a single Establishment.[30] Moreover, he has little of Marx's faith in the working class. Mills was, in short, a non-dogmatic revisionist (he admired the revisionism of Max Weber, for example) who called himself a "plain Marxist."[31] He used the term "plain" to distinguish himself from "vulgar Marxists," who dogmatically commit themselves to specific features of Marxian thought and identify them as the whole, and "sophisticated Marxists," who refuse to admit that Marx was wrong about anything and who mistakenly attempt to fit Marxist ideas, which are general theories, into specific theories and new sets of facts.[32] Mills tends to emphasize the humanism of the young Marx and places much less stress upon the inevitable march of history.[33] It is the non-dogmatic, humanistic, and "plain Marxist" features of Mills which make his approach attractive as well as a worthwhile and flexible framework for the development of community power theory. Mills, like Marx, has provided a general theory which can be related and made applicable to specific fact situations and to narrow-gauged theory; his power elite thesis cannot and should not, on the other hand, be made to account for all political phenomena despite its usefulness in the study of community power.

Urban transportation policy and its effects on the right of mobility provide an excellent example of a close fit between power elite theory and a set of political conditions which it appears to describe.

A closely integrated decision-making structure has managed to smooth the ratification process for the desires of the automobile-highway complex throughout the post–World War 2 period. The Department of Transportation and the Federal Highway Administration work closely with their counterparts at the state and local levels, and this is done even though it invokes the occasional displeasure of a transit-oriented mayor or governor (though there have been only a few of these). Even the busting of the Highway Trust Fund has been limited in its effects because the small amount of money which could be spent for transit has been administered by state highway officials or by highway departments now given the new name of "Transportation Department," which often hides the automobile orientation of most such departments. This areal structure of control provides great advantages and momentum for highway programs, but the functional integration of the automobile-highway complex is important, too. Slightly differing perspectives may be emphasized by one element of the complex—the AAA motor clubs, for example, or the construction unions—than another, such as the asphalt industry or the Associated General Contractors. Some of them, such as the auto-producing firms, have peripheral interests in the public transportation field and may, as Ford Motor Company and American Motors have done, express some interest in its development.

The major thrust of these functionally integrated elements of the complex is, all the same, never in doubt, and this structure strongly resembles Mills's "ring of establishments." This structure seems to contrast sharply with the groups which oppose the automobile-highway complex: the poor, the elderly, the environmentalists, the physically limited, and the transit buffs, who are occasionally supported in turn by a few ill-assorted intellectuals, the blacks, and other minorities.

The history of urban transportation policy has also rested quite obviously upon a narrow range of policy choices. From 1945 to 1970 only 1 percent of all government support for transportation went to public transportation.[34] The 90:10 ratio of federal support for interstate highways compared with a 2:1 ratio of support for transit systems, the automatic funding of highways compared to a normal appropriations process for transit and rail systems, the tax privileges and subsidies given to the automobile without question compared to the close scrutinization of subsidies for transit and rail systems, and in some places the absurd insistence that these systems must show a profit, the decades-long inability or lack of will on the part of Congress to set aside even a minuscule share of the Highway Trust Fund for transit purposes, the heavy advertising of the auto industry, and the socialization of American youth into car-using patterns of life with no real alternative, and many other public policy examples demonstrate the narrowness of choices perpetrated by the automobile-highway complex. A great many non-decisions also pervade the policy picture, and these figure largely in the kinds of personal decisions taken by individuals to fulfill their transportation needs: not to extend bus lines, not to build bikeways, not to subsidize certain commuter rail lines, or not to offer incentives for car pools; in many cases, as the Bachrach-Baratz approach to decision making points out, such decisions are never even considered.[35] Political symbolism has also played an important role in narrowing the range of policy choices. The Highway Trust Fund is described as a sacred "trust" in most of the complex literature,[36] car ownership is equated with prestige and prosperity, and non-ownership with poverty, a curious asceticism, or perhaps un-Americanism. Car ownership is falsely equated with "freedom." Mass socialization in the automobile's behalf also extends, in a curiously analogous way, to the economic arena and to the economic self-interest of individuals with much of the same effectiveness and some of the same effects as in the case of the military-industrial complex. Jobs are very much involved in the momentum behind the automobile-highway complex, with perhaps one-third of total employment in America reliant or partially reliant upon them. Those who oppose the automobile-highway complex and the misplaced priorities it represents are going to have to come to grips with this problem both in terms of economic policy and in countering the effective propaganda effort which can be organized around this point. This mass base of support is augmented by the massive scale of car ownership. Leading complex spokesmen, such as lobbyists for the car industry or the tire industry, deny that any complex or highway lobby exists, and in recent television interviews they have said that if one exists, it is in the form of 113 million people who own automobiles and trucks. Those whose mobility is threatened and/or ignored because of the centrality of the automobile in transportation planning and policy making are not to be worried about.

Systems-maintenance bias is baldly apparent in such statements and in the engineering and "professional study" processes which surround the automobile-highway complex. This is most obvious at the state and local levels. The illogical and outdated engineering premises which hold that "what we have today we will have two (or three or more) of tomorrow" show up in these stages of decision making. The havoc wrought by the Arab oil embargo in 1973 has only slightly mitigated this trend; it has not foreclosed it. The number of automobiles in this country has doubled in little more than a decade. It is therefore assumed that they will double again, perhaps in a little less time than that. Many urban communities have had to fight the plague of a "1990 Plan," which might better be described as a "1984 Plan," which inevitably provides, with federal, state, and complex prodding, for more and more cars.[37] This goes forward with little lobbying by the general public; they do not particularly want more expressways. The physically limited, on the other hand, must organize to a great degree of intensity, visiting HEW Secretary Califano's house and sitting on his lawn, in order to win a few guidelines that will give them not an equal chance, but a better chance, to exercise their right of mobility. In many of the "1990 Plan" arrangements, such as those introduced in Boston or in Fort Wayne, transit is either mentioned as a footnote or afterthought (usually in a "clarion call" format with no mention of financial support), or it is not mentioned at all.[38] One of the overriding considerations in the field of transportation planning, as in many urban fields of concern, is the unregulated and highly irresponsible "urban problems industry," which has used technical jargon and other obscurantist methods in selling its expensive studies to local governments. One of the cardinal principles operating in this industry, according to one of its spokesmen, is to use a lot of confusing and non-committal words and formulas in what amounts to a shell game. Standard paragraphs, brilliantly obscure in meaning, are computerized and fed into all kinds of reports on all kinds of urban subjects. The use of mathematics for the same purpose has been well noted in at least one transportation case study, and its effect, in combination with the other pseudo-sophisticated tools of analysis and obscure technical language, is to mislead and defraud the public and local government officials.[39] In a recent expressway dispute in the Midwest, a "1990 Plan" was found to be based upon traffic surveys which in turn were built upon and related to initial surveys completed in 1962. Since an entirely new methodology for traffic surveys came into existence in 1963, the survey data for this "1990 Plan" were essentially worthless. It should not be difficult to assume that consulting firms involved in such ineptitude care not a whit about the mobility problems of the poor, the elderly, minority groups, the physically limited, or the carless. Obscurantism, then, pervades the issue of transportation policy making much in the way that Mills describes its use by social scientists to promote status quo perspectives. It is one of the primary tools of the automobile-highway complex and its constituent elements.

The class dimensions of this issue are obvious. Automobiles, and most assuredly the complex, are instruments of the wealthy, the middle class, and special corporate interests. The transit alternative is still often considered to be, quite wrongly, only for the disinherited. An unfortunate circular effect is brought into play in some communities by this: transit is given crumbs, and this is seen as fitting since it is only for these "marginal" groups which are not in the "mainstream" of the society or the economy, service remains at an undesirable level so that the middle class is not attracted to the transit alternative, and the poverty image of the transit mode is continuously reinforced.

The Millsian power elite formulation for community power studies intrudes into transportation policy analysis at every point: integrated institutional structure, a narrow range of policy choices, a systems-maintenance bias, obscurantism, non-decision making, mass socialization, symbolism, and an important class issue dimension.[40]

Those who do not understand Mills's work often incorrectly assert that he was charging conspiracy against the power elite of the military-industrial complex, but he never believed that this was a necessary component of rule by the complex. For those seeking to understand the machinations of the automobile-highway complex, it should be obvious that conspiracy is not a necessary element for a power elite formulation to explain it; but in the case of this complex, we have it all the same. The Snell Report issued by Congress in 1974 tells a tragic narrative of General Motors's conspiracy against the transit industry. GM obtained control of a great number of municipal transit systems in the pre-World War 2 period by placing executives of a GM-owned subsidiary on their boards of directors. These boards, in turn, replaced trolley systems with motorized buses and later voted the entire transit systems out of business on the grounds that these were no longer profitable. More than seventy cities lost their trolley systems and some lost their transit companies—New York, Los Angeles, Philadelphia, Spokane, Wichita, Oakland, Mobile, Tampa, St. Louis, Cedar Rapids, Saginaw, Butte, Tulsa, and many others. Mayor Tom Bradley of Los Angeles has been fighting without success to establish a rapid transit system which would be only one-sixth as large as the Pacific Electric system which GM destroyed. This monstrous conspiracy was proved by the government in an antitrust case in 1950, and GM was fined $5,000 while the corporate official responsible for it was fined $1.[41] Though these wrist-slapping fines are an outrageous example of injustice, they tend to commend Millsian analysis.

Can a power elite approach to policy analysis be extended to areas of mobility policy other than transportation policy? It would seem so, for the plight of the cause of mobility in this country, especially when compared to other countries, is desperate enough to indicate that this is more than a matter of merely overlooking a deeply felt social need. Mobility decision making, then, appears to be formulated and dominated with elitist perspectives in mind, and those who cannot exercise their basic right to the fullest seem to have been deliberately left out of most policy considerations.

6

A CONSTITUTIONAL AMENDMENT?

No constitutional amendment can be lightly proposed, given both the problems of ratification and the gravity which most Americans attach to amendments. The weak position of the right of mobility in public policy, in American legal traditions, and in constitutional interpretation may still have strong enough roots in the culture and in the value system of our society so that the formality of an amendment could be unnecessary. Certainly that is the case with the right of privacy. It is not explicitly set out in the Bill of Rights, but a great body of law and libertarian protections have nonetheless developed around this concept so that many legal scholars, Justice William O. Douglas excepted, would contend that it has a sound constitutional position. Further, the right of mobility may not be enhanced at all by passage and ratification of an amendment. The history of the Constitution and of the Supreme Court is a history of various interpretations of most of the freedoms set out in the Bill of Rights, including freedom of speech, association, assembly, religion, and equal protection, as well as rights to a fair trial, against self-incrimination, against unlawful searches, and against cruel and unusual punishments. The Court, as often as not, has proved to be perverse, cantankerous, and unreliable, though the curious fact must be admitted that in our elite-dominated political system it is often the signal and single point of resistance against the excesses of governmental and corporate power.

Proceeding with a campaign for a constitutional amendment to ensure the right of mobility should never be undertaken until its proponents have developed a very clear approach to the issue. It has been shown that this right is often viewed merely as a right to travel or migrate, that it is sometimes mistakenly truncated to mere "access," and that some of its supporters would probably be content to leave out important considerations such as social mobility, the question of how to deal with no-growth or slow-growth statutes, or the rights of such groups as the physically limited. Some kind of general consensus on the definition of the right of mobility will have to be achieved among the proponents of an amendment as a condition precedent to the offering of the amendment itself. The debate on the right of mobility has probably not reached the stage, unfortunately, at which the aims of promotion and protection of this right are sufficiently clear to all its likely proponents and active supporters.

This should not deter thinking about the possibility of an amendment or about its aims, and, given the ambivalence which one must feel about the promotion of a constitutional amendment as a strategy for social and political change, it is necessary to set out arguments both for and against a potential constitutional amendment. First, there appear to be the following obvious considerations in favor of an amendment.

1. *An amendment would restrain excesses and abuses committed by governments or by others against the exercise of the right of mobility.* This would be the most important reason for enactment of this constitutional change, and it may indeed be the case that a properly drafted amendment dressed in the best libertarian prose could and would be enforced and interpreted in this way. But there can be no guarantee, and it is possible that similar or the same ends could be achieved through legislation or through case law developments. These alternatives take a long time, however, perhaps even a longer time than a ratification process would.

2. *An amendment would clarify the competing claims of the right of mobility and other human rights.* The *Golden* and *Petaluma* cases,[1] the various zoning, educational, and other restrictions against physical and social mobility that are now being developed, the impact of environmental questions, the role of public transportation in our society, immigration questions, including the dangerous prospect of internal passports looming on the horizon, the rights of the physically limited,

some tax measures, jurisdictional questions of state and local government, and many other issues could conceivably fall under the terms of a mobility amendment; but would they? And would clarifications develop or would there be more confusion? The right of mobility could be harmed in these "balancing" processes. This argument necessarily puts a lot of faith in the Court and its future interpretations. It also stands against a great deal of experience which demonstrates that the Court has not resolved any important clashes of constitutional rights and principles with one another. It has been very difficult for the Court to set up clear lines of demarcation between press freedom as balanced against the right to a fair trial, for example, or between the First Amendment guarantee of free speech as balanced against the right to privacy. Proceeding on the variety of mobility issues legislatively, one or two issues at a time, may yield better results and a clearer constitutional position for the right of mobility. Whatever the merits of this argument, the history of the law tends to militate against clarity of principles in the face of competing Bill of Rights claims, and this would particularly apply to the right of mobility, which, after all, is not an absolute right.

3. *Passage and ratification of an amendment would bring the United States into line with internationally accepted principles as set out in the Universal Declaration of Human Rights and would increase the international stature of the country.*[2] The latter assumption can be dismissed as naive; very little attention is given to such phenomena in the international sphere. But there is a solid point to the first part of the statement, for the constitutions of a number of countries, as well as the Universal Declaration, contain a mobility guarantee of some kind or another (see appendix). Perhaps the United States is seen by proponents of this kind of argument as filling some moral void in the world, particularly in light of the low esteem in which the United Nations seems to be held today. From a practical standpoint, none of this appears to be compelling; but from a moral standpoint, it is.

4. *A mobility amendment would promote development of the law; leaving the issues entirely up to the courts, or even to legislators, is not a policy at all.* The point here is simply that a constitutional foundation for the right of mobility would provide the courts with new guidelines which would enable them to develop new interpretations and innovations which, one would hope, would enhance and promote

realization of this right. What kind of interpretations could be expected must, however, remain conjectural even when we have the specific language of a proposed amendment available, for no constitutional provision can hem in the courts to any predictable pattern of decision making. Leaving these questions up to the courts, and especially to the legislators, it could be argued, is as much a policy as an amendment might prove to be. The probabilities are difficult to weigh, but in the face of such doubt positive action in favor of an amendment appears to bear the most promise of social and political change.

5. *A mobility provision would place a strong litigation tool in the hands of those who believe their right of mobility is being denied.* Certainly one can sue, can seek injunctions, or can make demands on writs such as mandamus on the basis of a constitutional provision, and it must be conceded that this could be very beneficial. Nearly all the cases set out and analyzed in chapter 3 would have been strongly affected by such an amendment, and surely some of them— the no-fault insurance requirement case, for example, or the suit by the woman who was required to have a car for her job—could be expected to have yielded a different result. Any suits under such an amendment would of course be taken up only by patient, determined individuals or rights organizations who could obtain the resources to carry such a fight through, and the results of such efforts are never predictable. This may be the strongest argument on the list, however, for a right of mobility constitutional amendment.

6. *A mobility provision in the Constitution would be a major educative force.* There is validity in this argument since an effort as major as an amendment involves a great deal of activity, fanfare, publicity, and debate. America is a society in which the consciousness of the authority of written documents is very strong, and this could lead to enhancement and recognition of the right of mobility in our everyday lives. It is possible, of course, that promotion of the right of mobility could also take place through more conventional, but not less time-consuming, means. A victory as symbolic as adoption of a constitutional amendment could be beneficial and, yes, educative.

These six arguments may not exhaust all the possible reasons for adoption of a mobility amendment, but they appear to be the best and most important reasons. Now consider some of the arguments that can be lodged against the strategy of an amendment.

1. *Mobility is already protected adequately.* This argument does not refer to the objective condition of the right of mobility in such matters as transportation, immigration, or the rights of the physically limited. Rather, it says that certain constitutional provisions—the equal protection clause of the Fourteenth Amendment and the commerce clause are good examples—have been employed by the courts, effectively at times, in the cause of mobility. It is conceivable that other provisions, such as association rights under the First Amendment or habeas corpus, could be construed to protect and promote the right of mobility. The present configuration of the precedents of the law and of constitutional interpretation, however, has important lacks and gaps, most especially the absence of any explicit right of mobility in any rule of law.[3] An amendment could fill such gaps.

2. *Constitutional amendment is a long, tedious process which in the end is still of uncertain value.* This argument has been alluded to in the discussion of some of the pro-amendment points, but it appears to be a solidly based warning. The history of American constitutional law demonstrates this argument well. The experience of the Equal Rights Amendment campaign, symbolically and substantively important as that victory will prove to be if it is achieved, also underscores the difficulties. Court interpretation of a mobility amendment will be both necessary and unpredictable, so that the simpler task of legislative enactment of the right of mobility in transportation measures, in elderly and physically limited rights laws, in taxation and in other matters relating to this right, may appear to be a more attractive alternative. This argument misses two points, however. The first is that no single legislative victory is probably as important as victory for the general principle of the right of mobility. More to the point, there is no reason to think that one cannot simultaneously push for an amendment and for measures which are in consonance with the principles of an amendment.

3. *Judges cannot be trusted to give satisfactory or even fair interpretations of the Constitution, and the potential of damage to the right of mobility through judicial fiat is even greater than it would be if individual legislative acts were passed.* Like the preceding argument, this one says that a lot of work could be expended on the mobility cause and could yield meager results. It perhaps goes farther than this, however, by pointing out that the mobility cause may be less vulnerable

if it can produce a number of legislative landmarks supporting this right in a variety of policy areas than it will be when it places all its eggs in one amendment basket. This tactical argument may be important, but it does not quite square with the way "real world" politics and governmental processes seem to operate. The institutions of government will respond to pressures at some point, and the intensity of pressure may be greater with an amendment or with the threat of an amendment. Again, it should be pointed out that it is also possible to promulgate legislation and an amendment simultaneously. Whether judges are fair in their interpretations is a subjective evaluation which turns upon individual perceptions and standards, although a mistrustful attitude towards judges can hardly be faulted.

4. *A poorly drafted amendment could do great harm.* Great care will have to be exercised if an amendment is to be proposed. Since the right of mobility cannot assume an absolute character but must include a definition of mobility as a process which covers a variety of human endeavors, complexities abound for the authors of such an amendment. Those right of mobility provisions which are manifested in a number of constitutions are not particularly helpful (see appendix). The variety of emphases in mobility literature and found among pro-mobility political groups—the elderly, the minorities, the carless, the advocates of public transportation, those who would reform development, zoning, and immigration law, and so forth—can complicate this task further. It still cannot be said that this objection is a very solid reason against an amendment. A well-drafted amendment could possibly do great harm, too, and a poorly drafted amendment might encounter good fortune. The point that care should be observed in draftsmanship is well taken; the point that this is a reason to avoid promoting an amendment is not.

The conclusion suggested by these arguments is that a mobility amendment, despite the tough course which has been outlined for it, is a feasible alternative to the present set of circumstances we find in American society. Furthermore, there are plenty of reasons, as outlined above, to believe that a well-drafted amendment could become a guarantor of the right of mobility. Pursuit of this amendment and of its enactment seems to be a more logical and promising course than leaving the fate of this important right to legislative enactments or the evolution of case law.

This does not in any way prevent lobbying and agitation for enactment of statutes of various kinds for the benefit of transit-dependent people, the physically limited, the minorities, the environment, and for the sake of social, economic, political, and aesthetic benefits accruing from the protection and enhancement of the right of mobility. How to go about this may be a subject for many more studies, though it is hoped that it will not become one of the subjects which are studied at the expense of positive and timely action. It can be seen that most legislative measures would deal with land use, taxation, and transportation policy and planning. These three are interdependent and should be developed in planning and in legislation so that they establish complementary standards and criteria. Policy making in these three areas remains hydra-headed, so that many of the benefits which might otherwise accrue in some stated land policy, for example, are vitiated by transportation or taxation policies or both. There is also to be answered the even harder question: who will have to pay for these changes and developments so that the right of mobility is enhanced for all? To some extent everyone will; but the heaviest burden can be expected to fall upon the wealthy, upon landowners, especially property speculators, upon suburbanites, and upon those who continue to insist upon using automobiles when other transport modes are made readily available to them.[4]

In vastly separated parts of the Western world—Britain, Australia, Ontario, Hawaii, and Vermont are good examples—there appear to be the beginnings of recognition of this interdependence of policies, of their costs and benefits, and of the right of mobility.[5] These beginnings do not amount to a trend; they are only hopeful signs. A constitutional amendment establishing the right of mobility would tend to bring these concerns together, joined in one general perspective on this right, one rubric of law.

A worsening of conditions for the right of mobility may also bring a constitutional amendment about, but this would be a signal that some great crisis in mobility had occurred, engendered perhaps by the adoption of internal passport legislation, by urban riots carried out by minorities or other disaffected groups, or by the unreasonable banning of migration to certain locations in the country. Before such events come to pass, it is hoped, we will have adopted an amendment.

7

PROBLEMS AND CONSIDERATIONS AFFECTING THE FUTURE OF MOBILITY POLICY

In all likelihood the issue of the right of mobility will be worked out on a piecemeal basis and in an ad hoc fashion. There have been no initiatives from any branch of government, including the courts, which would indicate any other approach. This is particularly unfortunate because the "closing of the frontier" mentality is now so strong in this country that it could lead to more immobility than now exists for our left out minorities and perhaps even for broad sections of the general public. Economic uncertainty, inflation, unemployment, land cost escalation, and a feeling of malaise stemming from the weak international position of the dollar and the knowledge that the Arabs can again close off our oil imports have all made themselves strongly felt in today's America. The general lack of confidence in government, institutions, the myths and shibboleths that seemed to work in the past, and above all, ourselves, has brought about a national atmosphere in which social responsibility and social welfare are given a back seat while we lose ourselves in various indulgences.

Such an atmosphere can beget meanness, and this has shown up in public demands for a harsh clamp-down on immigration, on mobility within metropolitan areas, and other exclusionary measures. Our elite-dominated decision-making processes are well established and well disposed to oblige such attitudes and demands. Land use and zoning decisions, transportation decisions, and a host of mobility-related decisions are handed down every day, and the trend of these is clearly against the right of mobility. There are exceptions: public transportation has been given a greater impetus in the years since the energy crisis struck, helping the cause of mobility as a by-product of an energy-saving motivation. The demands of the physically limited appear to have finally achieved some impact on HEW. The Supreme Court seems to be making progress, albeit very slowly, in the development of the right to travel, though not in the more general realm of mobility. These items seem to be isolated aspects of the mobility issue, however, and in no case does the cause of mobility make satisfactory gains. In the meantime exclusionists have found the environmental cause to be a handy veil for their motives, pass laws are being offered up as a panacea to the immigration issue, and many suburbanites who believe that they have climbed the golden ladder of success now wish to pull it up so that others cannot make the same ascent.

Whether policy decisions are good or ill, the fact is that they are being made all the time, so that the right of mobility questions are being settled and are being used as precedents for other decisions, judicial, administrative, or legislative. The right of mobility is therefore subject to a haphazard and ad hoc development without the benefit of its use as a unifying concept or goal of public policy. There can be no doubt of the deleterious effects of this upon the right of mobility, and we are now seeing some of the results one would expect.

There are some further complications. The right of mobility will not and cannot be effectively argued in the absence of vital data, and there are some important gaps in data collection and availability. We often have had to proceed in policy making without the benefit of reliable data because these are in a primitive or non-existent state of development. Immigration data, for instance, are described by researchers as "shoddy."[1] Some data have been privately acquired and are therefore not made available: "General Motors . . . has a planning team of systems analysts, economists and behavioral scientists. This team is compiling information about all American cities of more than 50,000 inhabitants, and has the largest data bank of urban information anywhere."[2] We need access to such data, a great level of sophistication in governmental data-gathering efforts, the establishment of at least one research center devoted to the right of mobility in all its possible facets and manifestations, and a greater attention to this area from research institutes and centers which are already in existence.[3]

A further complex matter we have not touched is the relationship of mobility and communications processes. Although access is specifically rejected as a substitute for mobility,[4] there is no doubt that the concept of access to services and needs and the right to communicate these needs and requests can have effects on the right of mobility just as the right of mobility can affect them. This was brought out poignantly by an elderly person who was faced with the prospect of termination of her bus service in the city of Fort Wayne. "I think I am being isolated from society slowly but surely," she said. "I will soon have no bus, I can no longer afford a telephone, and I feel that soon I am not going to be able to pay higher postage costs." She went on to say that she was being forced to stay out of contact with people for the convenience of this or that governmental policy or this or that special interest group. A powerful assault upon her dignity and, indeed, upon her very existence seemed to be waged against her, and the cumulative effects were almost more than she could bear. She needs help. The way out for her, and for millions of others, can be achieved only by understanding the relationships and the cumulative effects of the various policies and conditions which oppress her, and this calls for coming to grips with mobility and communications concerns.

Still another consideration, one which admittedly has been raised here but has not been handled satisfactorily, is the relationship of the social mobility aspect of the right of mobility to other mobility considerations. This question may be posed in another way: to what extent does the right of mobility depend upon a merely physical definition related to place? Any of the right of mobility issues—transportation, immigration, zoning laws, or whatever—appear to have a physical place question involved in them, but they also affect social mobility strongly and directly. Must there always be a question of physical place involved for an issue to be defined as one that concerns the right of mobility? It would seem so, or else the right of mobility loses its value as a unifying concept for a specific set of issues. Must questions of physical place or physical mobility be settled a priori in order to achieve the desirable goal of social mobility for those whose right of mobility is denied, unequal, abused, or threatened? Again this seems to be the case; but where is the line to be drawn between mobility issues and other issues? One cannot be sure without some reference to specific fact situations, but some issues—particularly the ones most often raised here—carry with them the distinguishing marks of a mobility issue. There are, undoubtedly, some social mobility issues unrelated to the right of mobility in a direct sense. Wage issues are a good example, or perhaps health, or most certainly some aspects of education, but there are no right of mobility issues which appear to be unrelated to social mobility. This is where this relationship sits at the moment, but more thinking and writing on this topic seems required and should be encouraged and welcomed.

In 1890 Samuel D. Warren and Louis D. Brandeis wrote a persuasive and well-reasoned article in the *Harvard Law Review* on "The Right to Privacy."[5] Brandeis went on, of course, to become one of our greatest Supreme Court justices. A great deal of the development of the right to privacy in America can be traced to the awakening of concern about it by Warren and Brandeis. The right to privacy was not then, nor is it now, literally guaranteed by the Constitution, but the two authors believed that the innovations of communications and press photography, among other considerations, had brought about a need for legal and policy recognition of this right. They set out the need for tort damages to be awarded to anyone whose privacy was invaded by another. The development of the law of privacy since 1890 has been erratic, some of the recommendations of the article are still not found as guidelines in the law, and the present-day status of privacy law has been called "a thing of threads and patches."[6] The Supreme Court has nevertheless forged a great many libertarian protections of privacy over the years based upon the penumbra of other rights specified in the Constitution, and these protections are vital for a free people.[7] The Court has similarly found that the right to travel exists in the Constitution, the absence of a specific protective provision notwithstanding, and as with privacy, it has interpreted this right to be in existence from the tenor and tone of the other rights set out specifically.[8]

These analogies suggest that the Court and other branches of the government can proceed with the protection and the promotion of the right of mobility, and that changes in present-day America require this just as the changes of 1890 pointed out an obvious need for the protection of privacy. Public policy, however, is never carried out in a vacuum and never settles down to a steady state. This means that the failure to proceed will surrender the advantages and the momentum to those currents and forces which inhibit and threaten mobility. Our times, our needs, and our people deserve a better fate than that.

8

MOBILITY POLICY
DEVELOPMENTS OF 1979

A number of significant events and policy changes over the past
year are certain to affect the right of mobility, and most of these
will mean further setbacks for those whose mobility is most threatened.
The energy crisis erupted in visible form again, with long gas lines,
strikes by independent truckers, demonstrations by farmers, and occasional violence, including a full-fledged "gas riot" in Levittown,
Pennsylvania. Allocation systems advocated by President Carter,
various state governors, and individual members of Congress all failed
to become law for a variety of political reasons. Failures of planning
and of leadership, consistent since the 1973 Arab oil embargo, are
now reaping a bitter harvest. The inability to exercise the right of
mobility is no longer limited merely to the "left out"—the poor, the
elderly, the inner city resident, and the carless—but now extends to
the relatively affleunt middle class. Suburbanites face the possibility
of being stranded unless they can adjust, and quickly, to the expedients
of car pools, smaller cars, and possibly public transportation.

The atmosphere is one of malaise and distrust. Pronouncements of
the oil companies, the Department of Energy, or of politicians are
viewed with skepticism or ignored altogether. Reliable data are scarce
and are mostly in the hands of the oil companies. The predictable but
hopeless search for a quick technological "fix" goes on, manifesting
faith in hydrogen-powered cars, gasohol, fuels derived from chicken
manure, injector systems, synthetic fuels, and new combustion techniques. A far stronger impulse is the public's belief that things have

gone terribly wrong, that life styles and opportunities will never be the same again, and that the "closing of the frontier" of American progress has finally occurred.

This crisis atmosphere is not conducive to the solution of energy problems nor to the equally great problem of promotion and protection of the right of mobility. The tendencies are those of panic and scapegoating. The energy crisis of 1979, therefore, poses two acute dangers for the right of mobility. The first is one of policy paralysis in the field of transportation; to a great extent, this has already occurred. The second is the threat of even greater inequity in mobility policy, a trend that has already been set in recent years.

The Department of Transportation spent much of the year pushing three of its favorite projects: Secretary Brock Adams's call for a prototype model of an energy-saving car to be built, a project which would lead to a major subsidy of the auto companies by the government; the Trans-Bus, a prototype public transportation vehicle which would eventually replace (at much greater expense) all busses in the country (the specifications for the Trans-Bus proved too complex even for General Motors, so that no bus manufacturer even gave DOT a bid for the contract); and the halving of Amtrak services when, coincidentally, rail passenger demand was achieving record levels and potential customers were being turned away in droves.

Urban public transportation, supposedly the centerpiece of the Department's concerns, was left to languish. The Chicago bus system was straining at the seams, and the same was true in cities large and small—Los Angeles, Dallas, Cleveland, Denver, Memphis, Nashville, Syracuse, Washington, Seattle. Public transportation systems now fear that they cannot handle ridership increases as small as ten percent.[1] In addition, public opinion surveys demonstrate an increased interest in the possibility of switching from cars to public transit. However, the Department of Transportation has given no indication that it can or will deal with this new demand.

This inertia makes the second danger—greater inequities in transportation—all the more threatening. The precedents for inequity in transportation policy-making have been previously set out, and they continuously show up in matters like the "averaging" of gas mileage capabilities for cars produced by each auto-maker. (This particular form of elitism rests, of course, upon allowing the owners of gas guzzlers to be profligate so long as the rest of the car-buying public observes economies.) The persons newly threatened by inequities as a result of the 1979 energy crisis are those who have not yet switched to public transportation, either because of choice or because of the nonavailability imposed by DOT policies, but who can barely or marginally continue to own a car in the face of ever-escalating fuel costs. The solution proposed for these people by the Carter Administration, the oil companies, conservative economists, and others is to let price become the determinant of who can, and who cannot, drive a car. Deregulation of domestically-produced fuel, it must be assumed, will produce hardship and immobility for those persons, particularly rural and suburban poor people, who are unable to use public transportation alternatives.

Replacement of the car by public transportation on a broad basis which encompasses all income groups is the optimal goal of any sensible long-range mobility policy; and, for that matter, this applies to energy policy as well. In the interim, however, it is important to make this policy shift so that as few people as possible are caught between high energy prices on one hand and non-availability of public transportation alternatives on the other. This means that there must be an allocation system based upon equity and not upon the so-called "price system." The most workable proposal developed to date is set out by Professor K. Robert Nilsson, Professor of Political Science at Dickinson College. He proposes a simple allocation of one thousand gallons of gasoline per family per year. Each family could use its thousand gallons as it chooses—summer trips, commuting, or whatever. Those not using their thousand gallons would be freely and legally entitled to sell them on a "white market" basis. The system would require very little bureaucratic intervention and control, it would penalize gas guzzlers and reward economic use of fuel, and it would provide an interim method which, hopefully, will be a landmark on the path towards greater public transportation development and use accompanied by the redesign of cities along energy-efficient, high-density lines. Professor Nilsson does not propose to provide carless families with a thousand gallon quota, but this would be a fair method of operating the system since we owe something to the families who have not wasted energy resources and who could benefit from some income redistribution. The "white market" could be administered by banks or the Post Office, which would resell the gas quotas to "salesmen, Texans and Marlboro men."[2] The Nilsson proposal, and others like it, do not, alas, appear

to have much chance of enactment; the heavy pressures are for allocation by price, the "world price," a price which spells immobility for
the poor and the less fortunate. One U.S. Senator, S. I. Hayakawa of
California, even has said that the poor do not require gasoline because
they do not work.[3]

Just as depressing is the heavy blow suffered by the physically
limited in *Southeastern Community College v. Davis*, handed down by
the Burger Court on June 11, 1979.[4] After all of the difficulty of
obtaining HEW Secretary Califano's agreement to enforce Section 504
of the Rehabilitation Act of 1973, the physically limited now find
the legal definition of "handicapped" to be severely qualified. In the
case, a person with a hearing disability was denied the opportunity
to undertake an education at the college which would lead to qualifi-
cation as a registered nurse. Her deafness was held not to be a sufficient condition for her to qualify as a "i.andicapped individual" within
the meaning of the Act, and her denial of admission was therefore not
considered discriminatory. This finding overturned the Court of
Appeals decision in her favor, which had been based upon confinement
of its inquiry to her "academic and technical qualifications."

It is difficult at this point to interpret the breadth of the Court's
finding in *Southeastern Community College v. Davis*. It seems clear
that the general accommodation of physically limited persons required
by Section 504—ramps, access to elevators and doorways, and so
forth—remains unaffected. Specific programs of colleges or of other
institutions, however, may now escape 504 requirements and the claim
can be made that the question of providing specific access to these is
discretionary. Further court interpretations or legislation will be
necessary, however, before it will be possible to delineate the rights
of mobility of the physically limited. The brighter future promised
for the physically limited by government enforcement of Section 504
is now farther off, and some hard-won gains for the right of mobility
have been taken away by the Court.

The right of mobility continued to face major hurdles in housing
and development policy in 1979. A continuation of such zoning
practices as no-growth and slow-growth ordinances, minimum lot
sizes, bans on multi-family housing, sequential development schemes,
and a variety of anti-integration building code regulations make it
nearly impossible for disadvantaged groups to move to suburban communities. Two small policy shifts by the Department of Housing and

Urban Development, however, contain the potential for a greater affirmative action emphasis with respect to suburban housing, and with this, the right of mobility may be enhanced. The National Committee Against Discrimination in Housing, a Washington-based interest group, is pressuring HUD to expand two of its barely-used programs—known as HAP (Housing Assistance Plan) and HOP (Housing Opportunity Plan)—in order to make affirmative action in housing a reality.[5]

HAP is a program which has presumably cleared the barriers of the Burger Court because it is in part an outgrowth of the Court's decision in *Hills v. Gautreaux* (1976).[6] HOP may also surmount these barriers—though one should hardly wager on it—because its implementation requires a request for participation by the metropolitan area in which it is to be established.

A Housing Assistance Plan, or HAP, must be filed with a city's application for funds under the Community Development Block Grant Program. This is the major HUD program, one which has emerged from an amalgamation of a number of older programs, including Model Cities, public housing, and Section 235 grants.[7] The key provision in the HAP Plan which promotes the right of mobility is the "expected-to-reside" figure which must be filed. This figure is an index which takes account of the number of minority members in the community who can be expected to reside there in conjunction with the number of employment opportunities which are planned for the community.[8] Failure to include "expected-to-reside" goals is a violation of the 1974 Housing and Community Development Act. None of this, of course, assures access to suburban communities for minorities, but in Chicago, the site of the *Hills v. Gautreaux* litigation, the "expected-to-reside" requirement is enforced by court order and, most importantly, has been amended to include Chicago suburbs as well as the city itself. Originally, the *Gautreaux* case centered upon the Chicago Housing Authority and its sabotaging of fair housing plans within the city only, but these plans, which call for the construction of public housing units in previously all-white communities, have now been extended by HUD to the entire local housing market.[9] HAP plans have also been used, mostly unsuccessfully, to promote minority access to the suburbs in the Philadelphia, Detroit, and Hartford metropolitan areas.[10] At the present time, the requirement of HAP "expected-to-reside" goals is the most direct and usable approach for promoting the right of mobility in the form of minority access to the suburbs. Its major deficiency is the possibility—often the probability—of its non-enforcement. In the case of the Chicago area, a vigorous enforcement of the HAP Plan has been brought about because of the direct effects of Supreme Court litigation; but the expense of the program of placement of minority persons and families into suburban locations has appeared to make HUD reluctant to broaden the program.

The Housing Opportunity Plan, or HOP, also promotes minority access to the suburbs directly. The Plan requires metropolitan areas opting for it to draw up a dispersal program which will insure that desegregation occurs in housing on a metro-wide basis. The HUD award will be to the housing units which represent "assisted housing" in the suburbs. The Plan also involves solicitation of individuals from the local housing authority's waiting list, from real estate people, and from social workers. To date, there has been very little application of HOP, presumably because of the fractured structure of metropolitan governments and perhaps because of political pressures which have been generated against it in the same way these have been generated against all minority access mechanisms and against the right of mobility when it is to be exercised by the poor, by minorities, and by disadvantaged groups.

HAP and HOP both contain the potential, however, of broader application and if this should occur, they could prove to be strong instruments in support of the right of mobility. It is fair to ask why there should be any further promotion of suburban residency by any groups, since energy imperatives and even the process of suburbanization itself tend to have long-range effects which are detrimental to the right of mobility; but individual choices must be given as wide a berth as possible and seem to be only legitimately manageable through systems of incentives and disincentives. The present situation which obtains is one in which free choice is often beyond question because of the ghetto-ization of metropolitan areas.

Greater involvement of government in housing and urban development also is taking place at the state level. In California, the new urban program proposed by Governor Jerry Brown includes a proposal to develop serviced, vacant land in existing communities rather than the development of adjacent land, and the eventual banning of leapfrog development which has so adversely affected minority access and the right of mobility in the past.[11] In Massachusetts, a similar plan to control sprawl growth, combined with a flexibility in implementation of federal urban programs, is expected to yield similar patterns and results. The control of growth in an urban area does not therefore necessarily mean the establishment of barriers against settlement by blacks and other minorities with aims of residential exclusivity; it can mean greater access. It all depends, in short, upon how it is done.

Most other developments in the mobility policy arena in 1979 involved inertia at best and setbacks at the worst. The response to illegal immigration remained as shrill and xenophobic as ever, although some new research efforts were beginning to debunk some of the myths about the numbers of illegal immigrants, their taxpaying contributions, and their position in the work force. The structure of government, especially at the local level, continued to present major obstacles to mobility. A conservative mood in the country, an emphasis upon budget-cutting and upon some false economies, and an atmosphere of malaise and distrust towards government—and towards institutions in general—seemed to take the center stage of American politics in 1979. None of these developments make the right of mobility a less urgent cause nor a less necessary social need.

APPENDIX

Constitutional Provisions on Mobility

Universal Declaration of Human Rights:

"Article 13. (1) Everyone has the right of freedom of movement and residence within the borders of each state.

(2) Everyone has the right to leave any country, including his own, and return to his country."

—From *Everyman's United Nations,* 8th ed.
(New York: United Nations, 1968), pp. 587–88

Constitution of Ghana:

"Section 13 (1).... subject to such restrictions as may be necessary for preserving public order, morality or health, no person shall be deprived of freedom of religion or speech, of the right to move and assemble without hindrance or the right of access to courts of law."

—David E. Apter, *Ghana in Transition*
(New York: Atheneum, 1966), p. 378

Constitution of Japan:

"Article 22. Every person shall have freedom to choose and change his residence and to choose his occupation to the extent that it does not interfere with the public welfare. Freedom of all persons to move to a foreign country and to divest themselves of their nationality shall be inviolate."

—From *Constitutions of Modern States,*
Leslie Wolf-Phillips (ed.), (London: Pall Mall, 1968), p. 107

Constitution of Mexico:

"Article II. Everyone has the right to enter and leave the Republic, to travel through its territory and to change his residence without necessity of a letter of security, passport, safe-conduct or any other similar requirement; the exercise of this right shall be subordinated to the powers of the judiciary, in cases of civil or criminal liability, and to those of the administrative authorities insofar as concerns the limitations imposed by the laws regarding emigration, immigration and the public health of the country, or in regard to undesirable aliens resident in the country."

—From *Constitutions of Modern States,*
Leslie Wolf-Phillips (ed.), (London: Pall Mall, 1968), p. 140

Constitution of Sri Lanka:

"Chapter VI, Section 18, paragraph i: Every citizen shall have the right to freedom of movement and of choosing his residence within Sri Lanka."

—Joseph L. Cooray, *Constitutional and Administrative Law of Sri Lanka (Ceylon),* (Colombo: Hansa, 1973), p. 572

Basic Law of the German Federal Republic:

"Article II. (1) All Germans enjoy freedom of movement throughout the Federal territory.

(2) This right may be restricted only by a law and only in cases in which an adequate basis of existence is lacking and special burdens to the community would arise as a result thereof or in which the restriction is necessary for the protection of youth against neglect, for combatting the danger of epidemics or for the prevention of crime."

—From *Constitutions of Modern States,*
Leslie Wolf-Phillips (ed.), (London: Pall Mall, 1968), p. 28

Constitution of Yugoslavia:

"Article 51 . . . Limitation of the freedom of movement or abode may be prescribed by law, but only in order to assure the execution of criminal proceedings, to prevent the spread of infectious diseases, or to preserve the public order, or when the interest of the country's defense so require."

From *Constitutions of Modern States,*
Leslie Wolf-Phillips (ed.), (London: Pall Mall, 1968), p. 228

NOTES

1: THE MOBILITY CRISIS

1. *Shapiro v. Thompson,* 394 U.S. 16 (1969); *Edwards v. California,* 314 U.S. 160 (1941).
2. Families which own three or more cars now represent 10% of all car-owning families, while families which own two or more cars now are 45% of all car-owning families. Seventeen percent of all households have no car at all. Leo Bogart, "The Automobile As Social Cohesion," *Society* 14 (July/August, 1977): 10–15.
3. Bruce P. Hillam, "You Gave Us Your Dimes . . ." *Newsweek,* November 1, 1976, p. 13.
4. Letter to the author dated September 17, 1976.
5. Sandra Rosenbloom and Alan Altshuler, "Equity Issues in Urban Transportation," *Policy Studies Journal* 6 (autumn, 1977): 29–40.
6. Kenneth M. Dolbeare, "Public Policy Analysis and the Coming Struggle for the Soul of the Postbehavioral Revolution," in *Power and Community: Dissenting Essays in Political Science,* Philip Green and Sanford Levinson (eds.), (New York: Random House, 1970), pp. 85–111.
7. Lettie M. Wenner, "Setting Environmental Goals: The Distributive Effects of Regulatory Policy," paper delivered at the 1976 meeting of the American Political Science Association, Chicago.
8. Quoted in a review of *Nashville* by Richard A. Peterson, *Society* 13 (January/February, 1976): 93.
9. U.S. Senate Subcommittee on Anti-Trust and Monopoly Practices, *American Ground Transport,* by Bradford C. Snell (Washington: Government Printing Office, 1974).
10. Hannah Arendt, *The Human Condition* (Chicago: University of Chicago Press, 1958); Herbert Marcuse, *One-Dimensional Man* (Boston: Beacon Press, 1964); Jacques Ellul, *The Technological Society* (New York: Alfred A. Knopf, 1964); Theodore Roszak, *The Making of a Counterculture* (Garden City: Doubleday, 1969); Lewis Mumford, *The City in History* (New York: Harcourt, Brace, 1961).

11. Herbert Marcuse, *An Essay on Liberation* (Boston: Beacon Press, 1969); Charles S. Reich, *The Greening of America* (New York: Random House, 1970); Alvin Toffler, *Future Shock* (New York: Random House, 1970); L. S. Stavrianos, *The Promise of the Coming Dark Age* (San Francisco: W. H. Freeman, 1976).

2: MOBILITY: CONCEPT AND DEFINITION

1. Roger Nett, "The Civil Right We Are Not Ready For: The Right of Free Movement of People on the Face of the Earth," *Ethics* 81 (April, 1971): 213-14.
2. Nett, p. 214.
3. Ivan Illich, "Recycling the World," *Social Policy* 4 (November/December, 1973): 15.
4. *Golden v. Planning Board*, 285 N.E. 2d 291, (1972); *Construction Industry Association of Sonoma County v. City of Petaluma*, 375 F. Supp. 574, 522 F. 2d 897 (1975), certiorari denied February 23, 1976, 96 S. Ct. 1148.
5. Howard P. Chudacoff, *Mobile Americans: Residential and Social Mobility in Omaha, 1880-1920* (New York: Oxford University Press, 1972).
6. See for example the Tom Wicker quotation in ch. 1.
7. Jerry Jacobs, *Fun City: An Ethnographic Study of a Retirement Community* (New York: Holt, Rinehart and Winston, 1974), especially pp. 8-9, 35-36.
8. Anthony Downs, *Opening Up the Suburbs: An Urban Strategy for America* (New Haven: Yale University Press, 1973), especially the first chapter.
9. *Hills v. Gautreaux*, 485 U.S. 284 (1975); *Village of Arlington Heights v. Metropolitan Housing Development Corporation*, 420 U.S. 252 (1976); *Warth v. Seldin*, 422 U.S. 490 (1974), substance of case is in 495 F. 2d 1187 (1974); *Bradley v. Milliken*, 419 U.S. 85 (1974).
10. Universal Declaration of Human Rights, Article 13 (1) and (2), in *Everyman's United Nations*, 8th ed. (New York: United Nations, 1968), pp. 587-88.
11. Countries which have a right of mobility or travel written into their constitutions include Ghana, Japan, Mexico, Sri Lanka, Yugoslavia, and the German Federal Republic (West Germany). Great Britain has no written constitution, but has recently developed legislation for the elderly and the physically limited which is described by the term "right of mobility."
12. H.R. 8094 and H.R. 8452 (95th Congress); *Congressional Record*, p. H1902 (March 9, 1977); also an editorial by Congressman Robert K. Dornan, *Los Angeles Times*, September 4, 1977.
13. *International Herald Tribune*, June 16, 1976.
14. Edward C. Banfield, *The Unheavenly City* (Boston: Little, Brown, 1970); *The Unheavenly City Revisited*, rev. ed. (Boston: Little, Brown, 1974).
15. "Right to Travel: Quest for a Constitutional Source," *Rutgers Camden Law Journal* 6 (summer, 1974): 122-43.
16. Nett, pp. 212-27.
17. This would tend to mitigate some of the effects of the inertia of the legal system, i.e., rights must be demanded before courts can do anything about them.
18. *Changing Directions: The Report of the Independent Commission on Transport* (London: Coronet, 1974), p. 106.
19. Two recent studies are K. H. Schaeffer and Elliott Sclar, *Access for All: Transportation and Urban Growth* (Baltimore: Penguin, 1976), and Wilfred Owen, *The Accessible City* (Washington: Brookings Institution, 1972).
20. 394 U.S. 16 (1969).

3: THE LEGAL AND CONSTITUTIONAL POSITION

1. There is an enormous literature on privacy; one good starting point is Arthur R. Miller, *The Assault on Privacy* (Ann Arbor: University of Michigan Press, 1971); another is Alan F. Westin, *Privacy and Freedom* (New York: Atheneum, 1967).

2. Much of this point of view is found in E. F. Schumacher, *Small Is Beautiful: Economics As If People Mattered* (New York: Harper and Row, 1973).

3. There is a great deal of literature, especially popular literature, on this topic; an example is Leonard Gross, "The Best Cities in the West," *New West* 2 (December 5, 1977): 19–40.

4. The spatial dimensions of political and urban research are increasingly focused upon. John Freidmann, "The Spatial Organization of Power in the Development of Urban Systems," *Comparative Urban Research* 1, no. 2 (1972): 5–42; Jean LaPonce, "Spatial Archetypes and Political Perceptions," *American Political Science Review* 69 (March, 1975): 11–20.

5. Zechariah Chafee, Jr., *Three Human Rights in the Constitution of 1787* (Lawrence: University of Kansas Press, 1956), p. 168.

6. Ibid., p. 165.

7. *Hills v. Gautreaux*, 485 U.S. 284 (1975); *Village of Arlington Heights v. Metropolitan Housing Development Corporation*, 420 U.S. 252 (1976); *Warth v. Seldin*, 422 U.S. 490 (1974), 495 F. 2d 1187 (1974).

8. Quoted in Chafee, p. 173.

9. Magna Carta, 16 John (1215), c. 41–42.

10. 1 *Blackstone's Commentaries* 134 (Boston: Beacon Press ed., 1962).

11. Article 4; James I. Clark and Robert V. Remini, *We the People: A History of the U. S.* (Beverly Hills: Glencoe, 1975), p. A-2.

12. Article 4; Clark and Remini, p. A-2.

13. *Shapiro v. Thompson*, 394 U.S. 618 (1969).

14. "The Right to Travel: Quest for a Constitutional Source," *Rutgers Camden Law Journal* 6 (summer, 1974): 122–43.

15. *Edwards v. California*, 314 U.S. 160 (1941). The concurrence written by Justices Douglas and Jackson opposes tacking this human right to the commerce clause.

16. *Shapiro v. Thompson.*

17. *U.S. v. Wheeler*, 254 U.S. 281 (1920), overruled by *U.S. v. Guest*, 383 U.S. 745 (1966). *Korematsu v. U.S.*, 323 U.S. 214 (1944), has never been overruled, although this case involved use of the war powers.

18. Stewart A. Baker, "A Strict Scrutiny of the Right to Travel," *UCLA Law Review* 22 (June, 1975): 1129–60; Victoria C. Heldman, "The Right to Travel: Judicial Curiosity or Practical Tool?" *Journal of Urban Law* 52 (spring, 1975): 749–66.

19. *Dunn v. Blumstein*, 405 U.S. 330 (1972); *Memorial Hospital v. Maricopa County*, 415 U.S. 250 (1974); *Construction Industry Association v. City of Petaluma*, 522 F. 2d 897 (1975).

20. Heldman, p. 766.

21. "Right to Travel: Quest for a Constitutional Source," p. 122.

22. Heldman, p. 749.

23. 394 U.S. 618 (1969).

24. 415 U.S. 250.

25. 405 U.S. 330.

26. See the district court decision of *Construction Industry Association v. City of Petaluma*, 375 F. Supp. 574 (1974), which is overruled, 522 F. 2d 897 (1975), certiorari denied February 23, 1976, 96 S. Ct. 1148. Communities which provide a modicum of low-income housing and meet certain other requirements can escape any imposition of the right to travel argument; also see *Golden v. Planning Board*, 285 N.E. 2d 291 (1972).

27. *Sosna v. State of Iowa*, 419 U.S. 393 (1975); *Lawrence V. Oakes*, 361 F. Supp. 432 (1973).

28. *In re May Barcomb*, 315 A. 2d 476 (1974); *Shavers v. Kelley*, Civil no. 73-248-068-Z (Wayne County [Mich.] Circuit Court, May 20, 1974).

29. Heldman, p. 761.

30. Quoted by Heldman, p. 762.

31. 416 U.S. 1 (1974).

32. Heldman, pp. 763–64.

33. *Shapiro v. Thompson.*

34. Chafee, p. 165.

35. "The Right to Travel: Quest for a Constitutional Source," p. 123. Italics added.

36. See ch. 6.

37. 435 F. 2d 807 (1970).

4: THE DE FACTO POSITION OF MOBILITY

1. E. F. Schumacher, *Small Is Beautiful: Economics As If People Mattered* (New York: Harper and Row, 1973), ch. 5.

2. Ibid.

3. Ibid., p. 68.

4. Ibid., p. 73.

5. A small town in Arizona, for example, was recently the scene of conflict between older residents and young married couples who were moving in, possibly leading to demands for increased services and higher property taxes; a Colorado community sought to prevent couples with children from moving into the town because no schools existed in the community and one would have to be built.

6. See ch. 2.

7. C. Jack Tucker, "Changing Patterns of Migration between Metropolitan and Nonmetropolitan Areas in the United States: Recent Evidence," *Demography* 13 (November, 1976): 435–43.

8. *Los Angeles Times*, October 2, 1977.

9. Thomas P. Clark and Roger A. Grable, "Growth Control in California: Prospects for Local Government Implementation of Timing and Sequential Control of Residential Development," *Pacific Law Journal* 5 (July, 1974): 570–602; for a view comparing suburban development in America with that of Europe, see George Lefcoe, "The Right to Develop Land: The German and Dutch Experience," *Oregon Law Review* 56 (1977), 445-517.

10. The Rural Development Act and section 201 of the Federal Water Pollution Control Act are also providing important but skewed incentives in this way; W. Patrick Beaton, James L. Cox, and Ron M. Morris, "Toward an Accidental National Urbanization Policy," *Journal of the American Institute of Planners* 43 (January, 1977): 54–61.

11. 429 U.S. 252 (1977); 495 F. 2d 1187 (1974); 419 U.S. 85 (1974).

12. Michael N. Danielson, *The Politics of Exclusion* (New York: Columbia University Press, 1976).

13. Frank Schnidman, "Trial Court Voids Boca Raton Population Cap," *Urban Land* 36 (January, 1977): 24–25; *Construction Industry Association v. City of*

Petaluma, 522 F. 2d 897 (1974), 375 F. Supp. 574 (1974); *Golden v. Planning Board,* 285 N.E. 2d 291 (1972); *Village of Arlington Heights v. Metropolitan Housing Development Corporation,* 429 U.S. 252 (1977); Wink Glennon, "Santa Barbara: Limits to Growth?" *Working Papers for a New Society* 4 (spring, 1976): 36–43; *Wall Street Journal,* February 8, 1978.

14. Robert C. Ellickson, "Suburban Growth Controls: An Economic and Legal Analysis," *Yale Law Journal* 86 (January, 1977): 385–511.

15. Glennon, pp. 36–43.

16. Thomas P. Clark and Roger A. Grable, "Growth Control in California," pp. 570–602.

17. Kirkpatrick Sale, *Power Shift: The Rise of the Southern Rim and Its Challenge to the Eastern Establishment* (New York: Random House, 1975).

18. Roger Nett, "The Civil Right We Are Not Ready For: The Right of Free Movement of People on the Face of the Earth," *Ethics* 81 (April, 1971): 212–27; an example of racist literature on the subject of immigration is Edward R. Lewis, *America: Nation or Confusion, A Study of Our Immigration Problems* (New York: Harper and Brothers, 1928).

19. "Excerpts from Reports of the Comptroller-General of the United States," *Inter-American Economic Affairs* 30 (winter, 1976): 93–96.

20. Ibid., p. 94.

21. H.R. 8904 and H.R. 8452, 95th Congress; *Congressional Record,* March 9, 1977, p. H1902.

22. *Los Angeles Times,* September 4, 1977.

23. *Congressional Record,* March 9, 1977, p. H1902.

24. *Gallup Opinion Index* 143 (June, 1977): 28.

25. *International Herald Tribune,* June 16, 1976.

26. *Congressional Record,* March 9, 1977, p. H1902. Much of the foregoing discussion appears in Gerald L. Houseman, "Will the Social Security Card Be America's Internal Passport?" *San Francisco Examiner,* December 28, 1977.

27. *Congressional Record,* March 9, 1977, p. H1902.

28. Rehabilitation Act of 1973 (Public Law 93-112 as amended by Public Law 93-516).

29. Education for All Handicapped Children Act of 1975 (Public Law 94-142).

30. *New York Times,* April 7, April 11, and April 25, 1977.

31. Ibid.

32. Ralph Nader, *Unsafe at Any Speed,* rev. ed. (New York: Grossman, 1972).

33. Helen Leavitt, *Superhighway-Superhoax* (Garden City: Doubleday, 1970); John Jerome, *Death of the Automobile* (New York: W. W. Norton, 1972); William Plowden, *The Motor Car and Politics in Britain* (Harmondsworth: Penguin, 1973); Emma Rothschild, *Paradise Lost: The Decline of the Auto-Industrial Age* (New York: Random House, 1973); Ronald A. Buel, *Dead End: The Automobile in Mass Transportation* (Englewood Cliffs: Prentice-Hall, 1972); Kenneth Schneider, *Autokind vs. Mankind* (New York: W. W. Norton, 1971); K. H. Schaeffer and Elliott Sclar, *Access for All: Transportation and Urban Growth* (Baltimore: Penguin, 1976).

34. In many respects the automobile has little to do with transportation, and it is often pointed out that the term "transportation" is actually a pejorative when applied to an automobile in the used car business; a car must be much more than mere "transportation."

35. Public transportation was criticized by the chairman of the Tyne and Wear Road Users' Federation for forcing people "to sit next to someone I may not care to sit next to" at the Transport without Oil Conference, Newcastle-upon-Tyne, England, November 15, 1975. Survey responses given to the Fort Wayne (Indiana) Public Transportation Corporation include the objection that riding the bus

requires association with mentally handicapped people. Early Victorian objections to public transportation were similar: William Hickling Prescott, the American historian, noted during his visit to England in 1850 "how railways had broken down the isolation in which the landed gentry had lived. 'Your railroad is the great leveller after all,' he remarked. 'Some of the old grandees make a most whimsical lament about it. Mrs. ———'s father, who is a large proprietor, used to drive up to London with his family, to attend Parliament, with three coaches and four. But now-a-days he is tumbled in with the unwashed, in the first class, it is true,—no better than ours, however,—of the *railway* carriages; and then tumbled out again into a common cab with my Lady and all her little ones, like any of the common pottery." Gillian Avery, *Victorian People in Life and Literature* (New York: Holt, Rinehart and Winston, 1970), pp. 40–41.

36. On the use of the car as an instrument of suicide, see *Accident or Suicide? Destruction by Auto,* Norman Tabachnik (ed.), (Springfield, Ill.: Charles C. Thomas, 1973).

37. There is a well-known popular literature on this which extends into fiction as well as non-fiction. The automobile has long been associated with violence in films, for example, as in *Bonnie and Clyde, Bullitt, The French Connection,* and the James Bond and "Dirty Harry" series.

38. *Fort Wayne Journal-Gazette,* October 26, 1976 (Berkeley experiment); "Hostile Reaction to Traffic Project Devised by Planners" (Nottingham), *The Times* (London), October 20, 1975; "Diamonds Are Forever," *Time,* May 17, 1976, pp. 49–50.

39. M. H. Fairhurst, "The Influence of Public Transport on Car Ownership in London," *Journal of Transport Economics and Policy* 9 (September, 1975): 193–208; R. Stephen Barry and Margaret F. Fels, "The Energy Cost of Automobiles," *Science and Public Affairs* 29 (December, 1973): 11–18.

40. Thomas A. Murphy, "Bigness Defended in American Cars," *Fort Wayne Journal-Gazette,* May 1, 1975.

41. *Los Angeles Times,* October 16, 1977.

42. *Paradise Lost* and *Death of the Automobile,* both cited above; recalls have now reached record levels according to the *Los Angeles Times,* February 9, 1978.

43. *San Francisco Chronicle,* July 7, 1978.

44. Barry Bruce-Briggs, *The War against the Automobile* (New York: E. P. Dutton, 1977).

45. Ibid., p. 44.

46. Ibid., p. 192.

47. Ibid., p. 75.

48. Ibid., p. 31.

49. Ibid., p. 39.

50. Ibid., p. 68.

51. Ibid., p. 67. Bruce-Briggs also calls this GM scheme a "technical violation" of the anti-trust laws, on p. 68.

52. U.S. Senate Subcommittee on Anti-Trust and Monopoly Practices, *American Ground Transport,* by Bradford C. Snell (Washington: Government Printing Office, 1974). Also see ch. 5.

53. Perhaps the most graceless feature of *The War against the Automobile* is the author's unfortunate use of the term "deaf and dumb," which went out with pest houses and dipstools (see p. 26).

54. Barbara Rosenthal, "The Auto Option," *Environment* 19 (June/July, 1977): 18–24.

55. Alan Altshuler, *Politics, Innovation, and Urban Transportation Policy* (Cambridge: MIT Press, 1978).

56. *Gallup Opinion Index* 123 (June, 1974): 18–19.

57. Reported in the *Los Angeles Times,* October 16, 1977.

58. *Wall Street Journal,* October 27, 1977.

59. Ibid., October 4, 1977.
60. Ibid., January 31, 1978; Gerald L. Houseman, "Attacked, the Auto Gains Regardless," *Baltimore Sun,* February 16, 1978.
61. See ch. 5.
62. Joseph A. Ruskay and Richard A. Osserman, *Halfway to Tax Reform* (Bloomington: Indiana University Press, 1970), pp. 196–98. "Homeowners tend to view their tax benefits as a right," according to "Shaping and Misshaping the Metropolis," *Search: A Report from the Urban Institute* 7 (spring, 1977): 6.
63. *Washington Post,* September 17, 1978.
64. *Fort Wayne Journal-Gazette,* September 17, 1978.
65. For a new treatment of constitutional law and the issues of federalism, see C. Herman Pritchett, *The Federal System in Constitutional Law* (Englewood Cliffs: Prentice-Hall, 1978).
66. David C. Thorns, "Suburban Values and the Urban System," *International Journal of Comparative Sociology* 16 (March/June, 1975): 100–114.
67. Michael N. Danielson, *The Politics of Exclusion* (New York: Columbia University Press, 1976).
68. Nina J. Gruen, "In the Land Use Game, Who Gets the Monopoly on the Good Life?" *Urban Land* 36 (September, 1977): pp. 3–7.
69. Thomas Muller, *Growing and Declining Urban Areas: A Fiscal Comparison* (Washington: Urban Institute, 1975).
70. Anthony Downs, *Opening Up the Suburbs: An Urban Strategy for America* (New Haven: Yale University Press, 1973).
71. Ellickson, pp. 385–511.

5: DECISION MAKING AND MOBILITY POLICY

1. Two of the more important works of synthesis are Theodore J. Lowi, *The End of Liberalism: Ideology, Policy and the Crisis of Public Authority* (New York: W. W. Norton, 1969), and Robert Presthus, *Men at the Top: A Study in Community Power* (New York: Oxford University Press, 1964). Aggregates of case studies are developed by Morris Davis and Marvin G. Weinbaum, *Metropolitan Decision Processes: An Analysis of Case Studies* (Chicago: Rand McNally, 1966) and in some of the readings in *Community Structure and Decision-Making: Comparative Analyses,* Terry N. Clark, et al. (eds.), (San Francisco: Chandler, 1968); also by Robert Perucci and Marc Pilisuk, "Leaders and Ruling Elites: The Interorganizational Bases of Community Power," *American Sociological Review* 35 (December, 1970): 1040–56. Pluralist theory is set out in a great many sources, among them: Robert A. Dahl, *Polyarchy: Participation and Opposition* (New Haven: Yale University Press, 1971); Dahl, "Further Reflections on the 'Elitist Theory of Democracy,'" *American Political Science Review* 60 (June, 1966): 296–305; Dahl, "The City in the Future of Democracy," *American Political Science Review* 61 (December, 1967): 953–70; and Jack L. Walker, who faults Dahl for his de-emphasis on participation, in "A Critique of the Elitist Theory of Democracy," *American Political Science Review* 60 (June, 1966): 285–95. For a review of Dahl's many contributions, see George Von Der Muhll, "Robert A. Dahl and the Study of Contemporary Democracy: A Review Essay," *American Political Science Review* 71 (September, 1977): 1070–96. The list of anti-pluralist works is long and often meritorious; preeminent are Robert P. Wolff, *The Poverty of Liberalism* (Boston: Beacon Press, 1968); Wolff, Barrington Moore, Jr., and Herbert Marcuse, *A Critique of Pure Tolerance* (Boston: Beacon Press, 1965); *The Bias of Pluralism,* William Connolly (ed.), (New York: Atherton, 1969); Robert Pranger, *The Eclipse of Citizenship: Power and Participation in Contemporary Politics* (New York: Holt, Rinehart, and Winston, 1968); Isaac Balbus, "The Concept of Interest in Pluralist and Marxian Analysis," *Politics and Society* 1 (February, 1971): 151–78.

2. Douglas M. Fox, "Whither Community Power Studies?" *Polity* 3 (summer, 1971): 576–85.

3. Some of this analysis is based upon the perspective of two years of service as a member of the board of directors of the Fort Wayne (Indiana) Public Transportation Corporation.

4. James V. Cornehls, "Politics, Regulation, and Urban Transportation Priorities: The Triumph of the Auto Society," *Anti-Trust Law and Economic Review* 7 (1975): 69.

5. Alan A. Altshuler, "Changing Patterns of Policy: The Decision Making Environment of Urban Transportation," *Public Policy* 25 (spring, 1977), p. 184; this excellent article is recommended for a different view on mobility decision making.

6. "PAT Deficits: Big, but Not the Biggest," *Pittsburgh Post-Gazette*, June 30, 1977; "Study Finds Huge Waste in Subsidy of Transportation," *Fort Wayne Journal-Gazette*, March 18, 1973; Don Barnes, "Auto Education: On the Wrong Road?" *American Teacher*, November, 1974, pp. 8–9.

7. Russell Baker, "How to Keep Cars off the Streets," *Fort Wayne Journal-Gazette*, February 18, 1975.

8. C. Wright Mills, *The Power Elite* (New York: Oxford University Press, 1956).

9. Ibid., pp. 10–11.

10. This is well demonstrated in *The Power Elite*.

11. An example of the "musical chairs" routine in American big business (interlocking directorships, etc.) is set out in the *New York Times*, November 12, 1972 (Business and Finance section).

12. See Robert A. Dahl, *Who Governs? Democracy and Power in an American City* (New Haven: Yale University Press, 1961).

13. Mills, p. 342.

14. Ibid., chs. 12, 14, and 15.

15. Three pluralist writers, at the very least, have established such artificial boundaries: L. Vaughn Blankenship, "Community Power and Decision Making: A Comparative Evaluation of Measurement Techniques," *Social Forces* 18 (December, 1964): 211, said that for one to qualify as a "decision participant" it was necessary that he be a resident of the community at the time of participation in an issue; also see Linton C. Freeman, et al., "Locating Leaders in Local Communities: A Comparison of Some Alternative Approaches," *American Sociological Review* 28 (October, 1963): 794, and Edward C. Banfield, *Political Influence* (New York: Free Press, 1961), p. 9; both the latter specifically exclude participants who live outside the city studied and specifically exclude important state government officials who had a hand in the decisions studied. These three instances are pointed out by Roy Forward, "Issue Analysis in Community Power Studies," *Australian Journal of Politics and History* 15 (December, 1969): 26–27.

16. Fox, p. 583.

17. Kenneth M. Dolbeare, "Public Policy Analysis and the Coming Struggle for the Soul of the Postbehavioral Revolution," in *Power and Community: Dissenting Essays in Political Science*, Philip Green and Sanford Levinson (eds.), (New York: Random House, 1970), pp. 85–111.

18. Peter Bachrach and Morton S. Baratz, "The Two Faces of Power," *American Political Science Review* 56 (December, 1962): 947–52.

19. Murray J. Edelman, *The Symbolic Uses of Politics* (Urbana: University of Illinois Press, 1964).

20. See the readings in *The Bias of Pluralism*.

21. Dolbeare, pp. 85–111.

22. Thomas Dye and Harmon L. Ziegler, *The Few and the Many* (Belmont: Wadsworth, 1971).

23. *The Power Elite*, p. 244.

24. It is pertinent at this point in time to look back at the initial reviews of Mills's *The Power Elite,* for they reveal a great deal about that time (1956) and about many of the misplaced attitudes which account for some of the evolution of national and foreign policy. *Time* said Mills was "intellectually irresponsible," *Atlantic Monthly* that he was "obvious" and had a "tone of outraged discovery," the *New York Times* said the book was "an angry cartoon, not a serious picture," *World Politics* called it "utopian," *Political Science Quarterly* used the term "naive," *Saturday Review* held that it was "too pat, too patterned–and too pessimistic," *American Journal of Sociology* said "too simple," and the *American Political Science Review,* offering a number of epithets, among them "absurdity," said that the work was revealing of the "author's personal sense of frustration." These are collected in an undated monograph by Robert Martinson, "The Critics of C. Wright Mills."

Obviously, the work of Robert A. Dahl has been the major reference point when critics of Mills are listed and whenever pluralist theory is discussed, and he therefore is a frequent target of anti-pluralists; nevertheless, a close reading of Dahl will show that pluralism is as much an ideal for him as it is a description of political life, which in turn shows first that behavioralists are not "value-free" and second that judgments of his work should probably be less harsh since his focus is on what ought to be as much as it is upon what exists. In addition, there are a number of lesser-known works of Dahl, particularly on the subject of workers' control, in which he appears to be a strong advocate of this kind of social, economic, and political change because it is a goal of his pluralist ideals; see his "Power to the Workers?" *New York Review of Books* 15 (November 19, 1970): 20–24.

25. Lowi.

26. *The Power Elite,* ch. 13.

27. Dolbeare, p. 90.

28. Ira Sharkansky, *The Maligned States: Policy Accomplishments, Problems, and Opportunities* (New York: McGraw-Hill, 1972).

29. G. William Domhoff, *Who Rules America?* (Englewood Cliffs: Prentice-Hall, 1967), pp. 6–11.

30. Mills believed that three major rings met together–the military, government, and the corporate world–in patterns which were both confluent and overlapping. A general misunderstanding of Mills on this point has led to his characterization as a much more dogmatic analyst than he actually was; for example, see T. B. Bottomore, *Elites and Society* (Baltimore: Penguin, 1964), p. 34.

31. C. Wright Mills, *The Marxists* (New York: Dell, 1962), pp. 97–98.

32. *Marxists,* pp. 97–98, and Irving M. Zeitlin, "The Plain Marxism of C. Wright Mills," in *The Revival of American Socialism: Selected Papers of the Socialist Scholars Conference,* George Fischer (ed.), (New York: Oxford University Press, 1971), pp. 227–43.

33. Zeitlin, pp. 229–30.

34. William V. Shannon, "The Untrustworthy Highway Fund," *New York Times Magazine* (October 15, 1972), p. 31.

35. "The Two Faces of Power."

36. For example, see Chicago Motor Club (AAA), *Motor News* 63 (February, 1973): 1–2, 3.

37. Alan Lupo, Frank Colcord, and Edmund P. Fowler, *Rites of Way: The Politics of Transportation in Boston and the U.S. City* (Boston: Little, Brown, 1971), pp. 255–60, offers a critique of the Boston Area 1990 Plan.

38. *Rites of Way,* and *Highlights: Fort Wayne-New Haven-Allen County Transportation Study* (Fort Wayne: Three Rivers Coordinating Council, undated).

39. James A. Kalish, "Flim-Flam, Double Talk, and Hustle: The Urban Problems Industry," in *Blowing the Whistle: Dissent in the Public Interest,* Charles

Peters and Taylor Branch (eds.), (New York: Praeger, 1972), pp. 121–36. On the misuse of mathematics for purposes of obfuscation, see Lupo, et al., pp. 139–40.

40. Not all the important present-day symbolism of the right of mobility issue was discussed in this chapter, of course; for examples, the "closing of the frontier" perception and mood that is important to the mobility issue and which undoubtedly has some effects on decision making, and the no-growth symbolism encouraged both by altruistic environmentalist motives and by the desire for exclusivity in housing patterns.

41. U.S. Senate Subcommittee on Anti-Trust and Monopoly Practices, *American Ground Transport*, by Bradford C. Snell (Washington: Government Printing Office, 1974).

6: A CONSTITUTIONAL AMENDMENT?

1. See ch. 3.

2. Universal Declaration of Human Rights, Article 13 (1) and (2), *Everyman's United Nations*, 8th ed. (New York: United Nations, 1968), pp. 587–88. Also see appendix.

3. See ch. 3.

4. Anthony Downs, *Opening Up the Suburbs: An Urban Strategy for America* (New Haven: Yale University Press, 1973); David C. Thorns, "Suburban Values and the Urban System," *International Journal of Comparative Sociology* 16 (March/June, 1975): 100–113; C. G. Pickvance, "Life Cycle, Housing Tenure and Residential Mobility: A Path Analytic Approach," *Urban Studies* 11 (June, 1974): 171–88; Joseph E. Haring, Thomas Slobko, and Jeffrey Chapman, "The Impact of Alternative Transportation Systems on Urban Structure," *Journal of Urban Economics* 3 (January, 1976): 14–30.

5. Lawrence B. Smith, "The Ontario Land Speculation Tax: An Analysis of an Unearned Increment Land Tax," *Land Economics* 52 (February, 1976): 1–12; Peter A. Morrison and Judith P. Wheeler, *Local Growth Control versus the Freedom to Migrate* (Santa Monica: Rand, 1974); D. G. Murphy, "The Introduction of Land Commissions and the Future of the Urban Land Development Industry," *Australian Quarterly* 47 (December, 1975): 37–49; "Freedom of Travel and Exclusionary Land Use Regulations," *Yale Law Journal* 84 (June, 1975): 1564–84; "All at Sea with the Land Act," *Sunday Times* (London), February 29, 1976.

7: PROBLEMS AND CONSIDERATIONS

1. David S. North, "The Growing Importance of Immigration to Population Policy," *Policy Studies Journal* 6 (winter, 1977): 201.

2. Geoff Lacey, "The Dominant Car," *Australian Left Review* 50 (1976): 13.

3. This does not mean we cannot see currents and tendencies writ large in national policy and in our social fabric.

4. See ch. 2.

5. *Harvard Law Review* 4 (December 15, 1890): 193–220.

6. Arthur R. Miller, *The Assault on Privacy: Computers, Data Banks, and Dossiers* (Ann Arbor: University of Michigan Press, 1971), p. 184.

7. *Griswold v. Connecticut*, 381 U.S. 479 (1965); *Katz v. U.S.*, 389 U.S. 347 (1967).

8. *Shapiro v. Thompson*, 394 U.S. 618 (1969); *Corfield v. Coryell*, 6 Fed. Cases 3230 (1823).

8. MOBILITY POLICY DEVELOPMENTS OF 1979

1. *Wall Street Journal,* June 7, 1979; also, this statement was made by officials of the Fort Wayne Public Transportation Corporation.

2. *New York Times,* June 25, 1979.

3. *Time,* June 4, 1979, p. 69.

4. 47 *Law Week* 4689 (June 12, 1979).

5. Some of this information was provided by Ernest Erber, Director of Research and Program Planning of the National Committee Against Discrimination in Housing.

6. 425 U.S. 284 (1976).

7. U.S. Department of Housing and Urban Development, *Programs of HUD* (Washington: HUD, June, 1978), p. 2.

8. *Trends in Housing* 22 (November, 1978), p. 1; 21 (March, 1978), p. 1; 21 (summer, 1977), p. 1.

9. Interview with Ernest Erber, National Committee Against Discrimination in Housing, February 16, 1979.

10. *Trends in Housing* 22 (November, 1978), p. 1; 21 (March, 1978), p. 1; 21 (summer, 1977), p. 1.

11. *The Book of the States, 1978-79* (Lexington: Council of State Governments, 1978), p. 472.

INDEX